D1555757

Being Seen

A memoir about me: an autistic mother,
a French immigrant and a Zen student

Anlor Davin

Published by Silverxord Publishing Inc

10987 Rte. 322, Shippenville, PA 16254

(814) 226-6444

ISBN: 978-0-99143-693-4 (Print)

ISBN: 978-0-99143-694-1 (eBook)

About the Publisher

SilverXord Publishing, Inc.

Educating…Enlightening…Empowering

SilverXord is a small publishing company located in Pennsylvania. We seek to recognize, nurture and cultivate talented authors, musicians and artists of all backgrounds, and provide a forum in which their creative expressions may be accessed on a wider range beyond their immediate community.

SilverXord aspires to publish original works of quality across a diverse and eclectic range of subject areas while promoting advocacy, self-advocacy, health and wellness, and spirituality. Additionally, SilverXord offers a range of online forums, trainings, and tutorials. Visit us at www.silverxord.com.

All inquiries about SilverXord Publishing, Inc. may be directed to: William Stillman, Editor-in-Chief, wstillman@silverxord.com

www.silverxord.com

To the legions of broken-spirited autistic people of past,
present and future (hopefully less!)

Praise for *Being Seen*

"Anlor Davin opened a window for me into the world of an autistic person. Her memoir, appropriately titled *Being Seen*, is an honest, intimate sharing of her brave journey from a painful childhood in France all the way to Zen practice in California. Her courage turns misunderstanding of autism into empathy."

–Susan Moon, author of *This is Getting Old: Zen Thoughts on Aging* and *The Hidden Lamp: Stories from Twenty-Five Centuries of Awakened Women*

"From beginning to end, Anlor Davin's captivating memoir is a compelling read. It is at once tender and turbulent, but always honest and inspirational as it winds its way through the flats and pinnacles of life with an autism spectrum disorder."

–Liane Holliday Willey, EdD author of *Pretending to be Normal: Living with Asperger's Syndrome* and *Safety Skills for Asperger Women: How to Save a Perfectly Good Female Life*

"This book is a tale of remarkable courage, giving the world a deeply personal experience of growing up within the autistic spectrum. Unflinchingly honest, it gives us a perspective from human beings whose central nervous systems respond differently to the physical and social environment. There is much to learn here, and much compassion to be gained by reading this journey. Thank you, Anlor, for the strength to write this book."

–Richard Mendius, MD, neurologist, coauthor of *Buddha's Brain*

TABLE OF CONTENTS

ACKNOWLEDGMENTS

Innumerable labors and people allowed this book to come into existence and gave me the tools to be able to write, which is such a privilege. Though it is impossible to name them all –please forgive me if your name does not appear here -I want to give heartfelt thanks to my partner Gregory Yates and all those friends who freely gave of their time in order to edit my book: Hermann Clasen and Carl Segall. The grant I received from the Tarjan Center at UCLA National Arts and Disability Center allowed me to work for a short time with professional editor Doug Childers, whose sound advice helped me stay on track. Dan Gudgel helped me set up the blog whose goal is to promote the book. Last but not least, there are those whose support I could not have done without during my recent grave illness: Paulette Berger, Julia at SF Talkline, Marjorie Coombs, Lin Maslow, Manuela Piha, Annmarie Kokolios, many Zen teachers and students, for example the late Steve Stucky, my first Zen teacher. Richard Mendius. I also thank my publisher SilverXord.

INTRODUCTION

Are we ready to demystify autism? Each day and age holds its mysteries and autism is one such mystery of today. With each new book about autism, we learn a little bit more about this rather misunderstood condition and this book too attempts some demystification and dispelling of the bad press about autism. The title "Being Seen" is not so much meant to say that I want others to know I am autistic; rather I would like others to better understand the realities of autism.

As an autistic mother, immigrant and a Zen student, I feel a responsibility to tell what I have learned about autism. I want people to know what my autistic experience was like and it seems to me autism needs advocacy by the autistic people. Despite my challenges, I am in many ways quite privileged and my survival has been made possible by sustained peace. A disciplined Zen practice has allowed me to survive the terrible chaos and pain that autism is, and along the way I have learned to better (if imperfectly) express myself. I write this book with the hope that it helps some autistic individuals figure out what ails them. Many never do despite the improved knowledge about this condition. This is especially true among the adult population—after all it took forty six years and a serious illness for my autism to be seen. The bad press is such that of course we can't accept it to describe ourselves! I also hope that my book helps parents, professionals and all non-autistic people to better understand the autistic condition.

I believe that autism is just a variation on humankind: it often existed invisibly a long time ago. The increased intensity of today's environment renders it more visible and the increase in population may very well also increase its numbers. In countries with less intense environments (often more rural), there seems to be a lower autism incidence rate. At any rate interest in this mysterious condition has grown radically, fueled in part by the difficulties autistic people face in jobs, housing and other aspects of modern life.

Autism is a spectrum and I do not doubt that there are many who are tightly wound in it more than me, who may be entirely lost in a world of painful sensations and who cannot speak and tell us what they experience. No two stories are alike and my own experience points out that the degree to which an autistic individual is affected can vary overtime.

In order to describe the condition as simply as possible, when my son was a teenager I came up with an analogy about fish:

> Colorful and dart-like fish live in shallow waters and slower and often less colorful fish live further down at the bottom. Autistic individuals may be like the fish at the bottom, and neurotypical (non-autistic) individuals like the colorful fish closer to the surface. With their different ways and appearance, the bottom-grazers (at different depths of spectrum) can disturb and frighten the fish above. I am reminded of the octopus, whose alien appearance does not stop it from opening jars with a screw top on them and a crab inside in order to eat it, and performing other intelligence tests. Both types of fish contribute to the eco-system but the shallow-water fish greatly outnumber the bottom-grazing fish. Many majorities often believe that the minority ought to conform to its ways, however when forced to live in shallow waters the bottom-grazing fish are put under unnatural pressure and grave illnesses result.

For autistic people these co-morbidities may include depression, bipolar disorder, neuroses, adrenal insufficiency, low blood pressure, schizophrenia, obsessive-compulsive disorder, asthma, and many other possibilities. Unfortunately, these secondary effects are often taken to be the primary diagnosis.

Autistic scientist Temple Grandin writes that she "operates in a perpetual state of anxiety" but I prefer the word "nervousness." This is not to say I am not anxious, I am very much so. But I am first and foremost highly nervous and this nervousness reflects a primal instinct for survival, it starts in the reptilian brain and cannot be controlled.

My mind often starts by focusing on worrisome and dark facts, usually valid enough, but since the door that lets them in is broken, they may rather quickly create havoc inside me and I can't keep them out, I get lost in them, they are often all I see and focus on. If anger and aggression are reflected onto me, I might be immediately overwhelmed by fear, my brain will freeze and the only defense I can summon will sometimes be to mirror that aggressiveness, at times turning it inward and hurting myself in despair.

To see and appreciate the joyful side of things requires a conscious effort. Rather than try to make this nervousness disappear I must continually learn to embrace it. In this society of many distractions, the fast pace usually does not give us a chance to pay attention to the nervousness. The ensuing suppression may be manifested as physical or mental pain.

In order to be more accepted by people I learned to bend backwards and sublimate pain, pretending to all—and to myself first—that nothing was the matter. I have paid a great price in order to appear "normal." I have hidden my chronic agitation at all cost and various co-morbidities and illnesses started to occur in me. Nevertheless, I am fully endowed with the longings and desires of human beings, as a human being.

I sometimes think of a human being as like a body of water: Some bodies are calm, some are agitated. The cause of this agitation might be invisible, as from a deep underwater source. I do not want to be seen as crazy.

I am not. I am only different. I may well solve a particular life problem in a different way, one that might take longer but in the end may also be more thorough or even more valuable. We all have limitations and though yours are less visible, they are as real as mine. Even as a young child when I could not express it, I would acutely sense others' smugness. I have found that sensory issues are often the deep "underwater" source of my agitation. As Temple Grandin suggests in her most recent book, *The Autistic Brain*, "sensory problems may set off autistic behaviors."

I once wrote about how the world then appeared to me:

> *Traffic noise, slamming doors and ringing phones, people, loud laughter, TVs and radios*
> *Fragrances of all artificial kinds, exhaust fumes, laundry detergents*
> *Glints of moving metallic objects and scores of abrasive lights.*

Though from the outside it does not readily show, many situations overwhelm me into uncontrollable states. Like milk that turns bad or the anchor that is loosely tethered, I may experience debilitating meltdowns, tears and rages and/or do irrational, crazy things such as sobbing, screaming, biting myself, kicking, pounding with my fists or hurting myself. The two times in my life when I most visibly caved in under the pressure (which corresponded to hormonal phases: adolescence and pre-menopause), I easily could have been the one screaming uncontrollably as she is forced against her will into loss of freedom in an institution. It may feel to us, as it did to me, that we are like the wild horses being broken, that our freedom is at risk. There was a time when the doctors who believed me "completely incapable of rational thinking" would have easily been able to lock me away, especially when I was still a child and my parents did not know what to do with me. It seems to me that the degree at which I display autistic behaviors has greatly shifted at various times in my life.

I shudder to think of all the people like me who were—and perhaps still are—thought to be insane and locked away in institutions of various kinds or drugged out of their minds, who became the legions of "broken-spirits." For many of us being forced to live with others who do not understand our limitations means that sudden bright lights are flicked, vacuum cleaners roar nearby and we are never let alone—a kind of torture. Through sheer despair, pain, alienation and inability to communicate, autistic individuals too often commit suicide. The Simon Foundation Autism Research Initiative (SFARI.org) wrote an article on this subject entitled "Suicidal Thoughts Alarmingly Common in People with Autism."

Most all of us fear our dark side and if someone around us is often intensely dark this touches the darkness in us; in immediate and often unconscious fear, we will constantly reject and blame him or her. When any of us feel threatened, putting down, blaming, bullying or ostracizing all too easily appears.

Let us take a good look at our own dark sides and limits instead of focusing on our autistic child's deficiencies. The responsibility is not solely and independently that of the autistic child. Rather than your way it could be our "away" at times. An autistic child may be deeply hurt and overwhelmed by the message that she hears in our voice *and not show it*. I suspect that the belief – and all that comes with it – that the adult is superior can lead to a constant, subtle and slow clipping of the vulnerable autistic child's wings. From my personal experience, it seems to me that the autistic child feels this and can become, as I often was, very angry. In the other half of the picture, I abide with the saying that "it takes two to tango," I can't put the blame solely on the external environment, I too am responsible for these different ways of mine and anger is destructive for all.

Despite these challenges I immigrated, became fluent in a new language and raised a child. I suspect that many autistic individuals who are not cognitively destroyed are born with the ability to live and learn. I certainly do not know all the answers and have not figured out all about autism but I suspect that lessening of parental control and change of lifestyle for a less aggressive and more natural environment might often be extremely helpful. In order to overcome some of the autistic person's co-morbidities and signs of distress, a move to a quieter place and a radical lifestyle change may be necessary.

The following and many other questions can be asked: What physical environment surrounds you? Is it possible to avoid taking your child to the mall and/or other big crowded indoor spaces (hospitals included)? Are there many cars, trucks and sirens around? Is it possible to use non-fragrant laundry soap and lotions (including sunscreen lotions)? Are the rooms you live in too brightly lit? Is your child able to spend time alone and/or in nature? If you have to be in a waiting room, is it possible to wait in a quiet and dark place?

The nervousness in an undiagnosed autistic person may take an increasing toll on them as the years add up, it certainly was so for me, and the better way to reflect this progression seemed to simply follow my life's chronological order. Thus this book is divided into the three chronological major parts of my life, each corresponding to a geographic move. The best description I read in order to explain what happened inside me is about the General Adaptation Syndrome, or GAS (Hans Selye), when overtime, chronic stressors push the body in three different stages, alarm, resistance and exhaustion—it is not a diagnosis. I give an explanation of each of the three stages' reaction to stress on each the three book's part opening pages.

The first part describes my childhood and adolescence in France; life was chaotic but I did not consciously know why. Those around me noticed odd things but the oddities were dismissed as childhood quirks and people did not look into them further. In my preteen years my quirks were not so cute any longer. Many of the people who knew me did not want to stick around too closely and those who saw me for short periods of time saw little but bad manners and a constant scowl. By the time I was a young adult I often fainted and did not see the point of life, attempting suicide a few times. By then I had self-identified how to conform and hide my different ways in order to appear "normal." "Being seen" at that time was extremely dangerous to my freedom, and I resisted it with all my might. Without understanding my motives and in an attempt to escape the pressure, when I was twenty three I leaped for a radical change of lifestyle and emigrated, alone, to the United States.

The second and middle part of the book focuses on the twelve years I lived in Chicago as a young adult, when I had a son and was confronted with my challenges in many forms. While it was wonderful to have a child to love and care for, it also heightened my sensitivities. Chaos and despair often overwhelmed me, the stress on my nervous system kept increasing, unchecked, and "being seen" was still not viable. Nonetheless I kept searching for understanding. Fortunately for me, I now lived in a country where so many different cultures coexisted that being different sometimes –not always- passed easier.

The third part is a closure of sorts as I moved to California, stumbled upon Zen, became severely ill, and ten years later, and after some harrowing experiences, was formally diagnosed and properly medically treated. Ever so slowly my Zen practice helped me find a way to climb out. Proper medication helped me revive and I eventually started to enjoy life again despite my limitations. By then I was at an age where "being seen" and the many false assumptions that come with it did not hinder my freedom me so much.

Because I speak and write fluently in two languages I had the choice of writing this book in either French or English. I chose to write in English as more people understand English and it seems to me there is more open-mindedness about autism in the United States than in France. In my eyes it is telling that many photographs of French autistic children still show evidence of intellectual disability I have now lived in United States longer than I did in France and am more familiar with the words about autism in that language. Finally I want to be loyal to my adoptive country, where I have been able to survive independently and always on a tight rope despite my profound differences.

Here then is my story. For me, autism is so subtle it often is quite invisible and it may well be that those who read this book, encountering so many similarities with their own stories, forget that the book is about autism, that I am autistic. In the words of writer William Stillman, "autism is a natural way to perceive." Even if it is pervasive and results in many untold challenges, parents, professionals and autistic people alike can take heart, no one is doomed forever. If this book helps only one of us, or our parents, our families or our doctors, then I will not have written it in vain.

PART I

FRANCE, BIRTH AND YOUTH
1964-1987

General Adaptation Syndrome Stage 1: Alarm

During this stage, the body's response to a threat is a state of alarm. This is the stage where the body will produce adrenaline to bring out the "fight" or "flight" response. There is also some activation of the HPA axis (the Hypothalamic-Pituitary-Adrenal axis is a complex set of direct influences and feedback interactions among three endocrine glands), producing cortisol.

CHAPTER 1: FIRST FIVE YEARS

My mom, my brother and I (the crying one!) at the beach

My parents first lived in Paris when they met but my mother returned to les Sables d'Olonne, a sea resort, to be with her family for my birth, in 1964. My immediate family included my father, my mother, my younger brother and my older sister. There is much I don't know about my parents as they rarely spoke about their pasts. I think it is sometimes a "French way" to avoid speaking about the past and its difficult subjects, often making it a kind of denial.

My father was born in 1907 in Paris. He was an only child and I never met any one from his family of origin, I was told they were all dead. My father's grandfather, Emile Barau, was an impressionist painter of some renown. The few pictures of my father growing up in Paris as a child show him with unusual animals for pets: a lion, a bear and a monkey. He had a mysterious and troubled past, unknown to me at the time. It was one of those difficult subjects people were careful not to speak about, especially in front of the children. He had met my mother in a medical laboratory in

Paris where they worked together. He was fifty nine years old when I was born. Most importantly, I believe I have to thank my father for keeping me away from doctors and institutions when I was a child.

My mother was twenty-six years younger than my father and one of the youngest children in a large family of farmers in les Sables d'Olonne. Many of her extended family also lived there. She was expelled from her Catholic high school for reading *J'irais Cracher sur vos Tombes* (*I Will Go Spit on Your Tombs*) by Boris Vian and remained a life-long practicing Catholic. As a young woman she was the only child in her family to go away to Paris, which was a huge move at that time. She had a practical view of the world and a keen organizing sense. She loved to read, and sang in the town's choir (she still does). Though we mostly lived near many of her family members they tended to avoid visiting us, I didn't know why. My mother assumed the main care of the household and it took a heavy toll on her. Despite the adversity she managed to keep us in a relatively stable environment.

My brother is one year younger than me. As young children we were very close. I followed him everywhere and we were quite enmeshed as children. Such close contact often irritated me and we often fought like badgers, more so as we got older. My sister was my father's out-of-wedlock daughter from a previous relationship. She was a teenager when I was born, and a bond was created between us when she helped take care of my brother and me. But she did not get along with my mother, her stepmother. She left the family when I was about four years old.

When I was four or five years old we moved to Les Sables d'Olonne. The town is located in the West of France, near the Atlantic Ocean and about three hundred miles from Paris. In summer the population more than doubled with vacationers, many of them from Paris. The town's weather is temperate and its climate is mild, with lots of sun in the summers and no snow in the winters, and many older adults come to retire there. The *port de pêche* (fishing harbor) sheltered several hundred fishing boats. The fishermen often returned from their nightly runs to sell their catches wholesale first thing in the mornings in *la Criée* (the fish market), a lively scene of shouts, smells and various fish. In the commercial harbor that still existed then, boats unloaded grains and freight. Years later, this harbor was completely redone and became a pleasure harbor. The German bunkers left over from World War II were usually built on strategic sites overlooking large stretches of the Atlantic Ocean and there were many in and around town. The town of les Sables d'Olonne has become known worldwide for the Vendee Globe, a round-the-world single-handed yacht race ("regarded by many as the ultimate in ocean racing") that starts from the pleasure harbor every four years. This once-every-four-year race brings out even more crowds to the town.

Fortunately for me and my autistic hypersensitivities to noise and bustle, the town was often quiet, especially in the winter when the vacationers were gone. The blaring of the fog horn and the once-a-week town siren were the main industrial sounds.

During the school year many stores and houses were closed and after the summer. When crowds were gone, the town had an almost eerie, empty feel. We did not have television at home but I had a roof over my head, my own bedroom, food, clothing, an education with exposure to many extra-curricular activities, and basic medical and dental care. Shopping malls were not so big back then, and none of today's overly crowded public areas existed, save the popular beach during July and August. When the tourists were mostly gone and the tide was low I loved to observe the little tide pools full of mollusks and crustaceans. Every spring the soles of my feet grew painfully raw and then calloused from walking barefoot after my brother on the beach, stepping on the rocks and the mussels. When the water grew warmer, my brother and I waded in it under my mother's supervision. For unfathomable reasons, in my eyes and at that age—my father strongly disliked the sea; later I would find out he had good reasons for this. The cold, slimy seaweed appearing out of nowhere spooked me and often I ended up crying and screaming when exposed to it. I imagined terrible things hidden under the smallest patch and I went to great lengths to avoid it. My mother and brother found these fears odd and their comments were not always kind.

One of the first important changes our move from Paris to Les Sables d'Olonne brought about for me was in my living arrangement. The house we now rented had three bedrooms. For the first few months, my brother and I shared a bedroom, but another bedroom remained empty, reserved for my elder sister—who had left—in case she would return. She now lived in Spain and a few years later she had a baby daughter. But I vividly recall my sense of relief when my parents gave me her empty room.

Our house had a small enclosed back yard with one lone tree. My brother and I often played there, the dark storage shed on one side of the backyard was my refuge. When I was upset I sometimes crawled under the furniture relegated there to hug my knees and rock. I was scared of the dirty dampness, but though I did not understand it at the times, it was better than the alternative: the noises, the lights and the constant observation and criticism.

Nowadays I have little contact with my family of origin. Autism breaks many families apart and mine is no exception. My family put up with my oddity, not always skillfully. I often felt anguished and sad but at least my wings were not clipped and overall I was allowed a certain freedom to be. Because I was believed to be "normal," my constant nervousness and discomfort were not taken seriously. My recall of early memories is mostly from pictures of that time. I was apparently a difficult child, a picky eater who cried a lot and strongly reacted to my environment. My mother said I often calmed down during our numerous visits to le Bois de Boulogne, a large Parisian park. I do remember the bed my father made for me as a toddler, with its smell of fresh paint and my name inscribed in bright colors on the headboard.

My first memories are all of a sensory type. Perceptions and stimuli assaulted my senses, dominated my life and created havoc inside me. Despite my odd ways I was given many opportunities to live and learn and my freedom was never curtailed. However my hypersensitivity earned me at an early age the derisive label of drama queen. My parents told me I was like a *"chat échaudé craint l'eau chaude,"* the cat that has been scalded and fears all water. In their eyes I was a child who cried for no reason and almost all the time. Thus early on I took great pains to hide my distress. My hypersensitivities would not be diagnosed as part of my autism for many years.

CHAPTER 2: SOCIAL EXPOSURE AND ELEMENTARY SCHOOL

Another important change resulted from our move to Les Sables d'Ol-onne: with the frequent sight and presence of new places and people, I felt a kind of raw exposure that was often challenging. I already exhibited fierce passions and intense emotions - what autistic literature often calls "obsession."

Sometimes I pressed my hands on my eyeballs so as to experience an iridescence of colors, but I stopped when it hurt (I have heard of some autistic children who blind themselves that way). Many times I uncon-sciously scratched the skin near my right thumb nail to a bleeding and pain-ful point. Such behaviors are called in the autistic vocabulary "stimming." Despite the dictionary's definition about it as "self-stimulation" behavior I prefer autistic Carly Fleishmann's description—at about age fifteen—that "doctors have the definition of stimming wrong. Stims are when you make or create output to block sensory input or overload." (This quote can be found in "A Conversation with Carly," at the end of her book *Carly's Voice*).

Realistically I was fortunate not to be labeled; nobody thought much of my different ways nor was especially frightened by them, and no doctors were involved. I acutely sensed that others (for example my mother) felt I should think and behave in more conventional ways.

There is a culture of tennis in my family and my father was an accom-plished and passionate player who was introduced to tennis in the womb—literally: in my parents' living room hung a picture of my grandmother playing tennis in a long robe and a fancy hat, in the style of the early twen-tieth century and not long after the game as we know it today started. In that picture, my grandmother was late in her pregnancy with my father, but it didn't show as she was wearing a tight corset. By his early twenties my father had played with the soon-to-be-legendary French tennis players, the "four musketeers": Cochet, Borotra, Brugnon and Lacoste. Nicknamed "the Crocodile," Lacoste founded the clothing line with the famous crocodile logo. When I was five years old, my father became the tennis teacher at the Tennis Club des Sables d'Olonne; many people—including me—remember him bellowing out to his students "*un, deux, trois*" ("one, two, three") in cadence with the steps of the tennis player's forehand. While my father taught my mother to play, my brother and I explored the tennis club property. We built huts in hidden places on the untamed grounds, places where I sometimes ran in times of stress in order to calm myself in the dark and quiet. Soon my brother and I started learning to play tennis under my father's supervision. When my father saw that I enjoyed the game, he started to train me more often. The tennis club had a practice wall, where I honed my skills for hours at a time. I spent countless hours there, alone and enjoying not having to run back and forth while rehearsing the same move over and over. I loved the concentrated repetition and solitude of solo practice. I had to practice and repeat the same thing day after day, and that was regarded as positive, without the negativity of obsession. I learned how to remember left and right side by miming a tennis swing with my dominant left hand. Tennis is in many ways an excellent school of life, it certainly was for me. I have met or heard of many autistic people who excel in one focused discipline, either physical or mental. There are social and sensory reasons that make tennis a good activity for autistic children: tennis requires only two people and after learning the basics you are left alone on your side of the court. The relative quiet, the clearly delineated rules, lines and shape of the court and the intense focus on the ball may help create an environment of relative stability and safety.

Another type of social exposure in my early years was the Catholic Church in Les Sables d'Olonne, where my mother was the main secretary. Her office was located in the building adjacent to the Church of Saint

Pierre. This job provided the foundation of our household income and my mother kept it throughout my life in France. Until we became unruly teenagers, every Sunday morning she and my aunt took us children to mass. My brother served as an altar boy and wore special clothes. My mother wanted me to dress up too, but I hated the constraining formal girl dresses and we often fought before church. With my short hair and tomboy looks I could pass for a boy and once when my brother was sick I took his place as the altar boy. But normally I sat in the pew listening and trying to make sense of the priest's homily. Sometimes I went up to the pulpit and read biblical passages into the microphone.

The biblical recommendation to "turn the other cheek" intrigued me. I reflected much over it and tried to act accordingly. I understood the passage to mean that allowing one's self to be more vulnerable would bring peace, so I made myself more vulnerable by trying to share with others the pain caused by sensations and perceptions. But my efforts were not comprehended, I found no peace and I concluded that my understanding was faulty. Eventually I realized that one could not "turn the other cheek" without first being strong enough to withstand the results. Later, as an adult, I also realized that I clearly was not always so strong. Many autistic people seem to have a profoundly idealistic streak that may emerge from their fundamental lack of guile.

When I started to go to school it was a new type of discomfort for me as I was not used to be restrained indoor with many others. The Sainte Therese grammar school was Catholic, which for me never meant anything other than having to wear a smock my aunt had sewed (she was an accomplished seamstress and sewed many of our clothes); and this was convenient as it meant that I did not need to plan ahead the clothes I would be wearing the next day. I skipped the first grade. The reason for this was never discussed with me aloud, but it most likely was due to my unusual reading abilities. I have no memory of how I learned to read on my own before kindergarten but I suspect it had to do with the kind of mental decoding with written words—something I often excel at. The good thing is that, for most of my childhood, my inordinate reading ability warded away the label of mental retardation. I also remember myself as the typical "little professor," talking non-stop (a cover up) about non age-related topics, a common autistic characteristic. Thanks to these first skills, my parents respected me.

I disliked going to school and I was extremely disappointed that my mother never kept me home during a school day. Desperate, I once made up a story that the school was closed for vacation for a few days. It was the very first fib I ever told my mother, and when she found out her anger left me paralyzed with fright. After this I hardly ever missed a day in school or other activities, and remained the same until being much older. In my eyes, this incident was the conscious beginning of the gap between my mother and me. I was so sad that she did not "get me," she did not understand my world and I could not trust her about it. The gulf between us would only grow bigger and wider every day.

In order to teach the multiplication table, the teacher made the class say it aloud every day. In my case it worked; the multiplication tables became a tune I can still remember: "*une fois un fait un, une fois deux font deux, une fois trois [font] trois...*" all the way to "ten by ten make a hundred."

It was a challenge to learn how to write and at first my penmanship was a mess. I did not follow the lines and I stained the paper with the ink from the quill that dragged under my hand. Despite the fact that my dominant hand is the left, the teacher believed I ought to write with my right hand and my mother had to come in person to confront her to allow me to use my left hand. This was for me a proof of my mother's care, a rare event and I cherished it. I was not about to let her down, I struggled hard and in time I did learn to write clearly. Since then, I have often been complimented about my handwriting!

My brother and I had lunch at school and for me those meals soon became yet another challenge. The head cook of the lunchroom was the same teacher with whom I already had penmanship difficulties. I perceived her as mean and I felt forced to eat the foods she had prepared, lunch soon became a nightmare and I hardly ate. No wonder I was so thin at that age, I was so skinny my parents thought I must have a worm inside me.

I was in the same class as the babysitter's younger sister (I think she was the only babysitter—other than my older sister—we ever had and it did not last very long). Thus I did not have to initiate the first contact and for the next ten years Marie and I became best friends. We started to do many things together. In elementary school during a recess walk around the school yard the headmaster reprimanded us; she said we were holding arms in a way that made us look as if we were old people. This incident was one of the many instances that left me confused and frightened.

I was thought to be unusually gifted, though in an extraordinary way. I processed things differently than most, but once I processed them, often in a mysterious, slow and unexplained way, what I had learned was thorough. Though I did not understand how exactly to do it, I struggled to appear to behave like the others. I had started to figure how useless it was to tell my mother how scared and nervous I was. I was just another child, with likes and dislikes, trying to make sense of the world around her. I am so fortunate I managed to keep the most troublesome and different behaviors in check while in school, only to act out at home. What is sometimes understood as "slowness" in autistic children and adults may simply be a different way of processing. Assessments by people who did not understand me, but assumed they did and felt superior, painfully exacerbated my vulnerability and the fragility of my nervous system.

CHAPTER 3: A SENSITIVE CHILD WITH A NEED FOR MUCH ACTIVITY

Is a worm making me so skinny? - Circa 1971

Covering up for the inexplicable stress I felt was a major constant. Instinctively, I knew that if I did not do a good enough job of pretending, I would not appear "normal" and would be labeled. When this constant pressure inside me caused various ailments (for example constipation) and different behaviors, I was told that my imagination was the culprit. Repressions and compensations became my second nature at an early age.

When I was about eight years old, during a drive to work before dawn, my father had a car accident. He said he had fallen asleep at the wheel. The car had careened into a nearby tree, which became for me an "emotional landmark." During the next ten years, each time I drove by the tree and saw its scar, I was upset. The car overturned on my father's Achilles tendon, and it was a long time before he was found, unconscious. Once emergency medical care had been completed, he adamantly refused to further see doctors for any kind of rehabilitation. After the accident he was forever unable to run and limped. My mother suspected he had tried to kill himself with this accident. Years later, she told me that he eventually admitted this to her. In any event, to my childlike eyes, he was never the same afterwards, he rarely laughed heartily again, nor brought flowers and other gifts to my mother.

When my father had to dress up on rare and grave occasions, he put on his lavender cologne. The smell of it strongly affected me and at those times I stayed away from my father; however I took this strong reaction to mean that I liked the smell. It is only as an older adult that I understood how such artificial and strong smells affected me negatively. I know from this experience that children and young people can have strong aversions of which they are not consciously aware.

Once, when my brother and I were running with friends away from the tennis club gardener after a prank, we had to jump down from a high fence. I was last and stayed paralyzed with fear on top of the fence. I knew from previous experiences that upon landing sometimes my knees would painfully lock, and that when this happened I was likely to injure myself. Forced to make a move for fear of the approaching gardener, I finally jumped. I fell and twisted my ankle, but thankfully not enough to keep me from following after the others, who had by then disappeared from view. After having mulled over this incident for a while, the child I was realized –but did not tell anyone as I would not have known how to express this- that when I was nervous my "landing reflex" was impaired. There were other times where, with no time to think it over and no nervousness inside me, the reflex came naturally –for example during my gymnastics classes.

One night my brother and I were alone at home as my parents were (if I remember correctly) playing bridge with friends. I woke up with a terrible feeling of dread and I could not go back to sleep. Eventually I ventured to get up and woke up my brother, whose bedroom was next door. He was angry with me but the two of us went downstairs to check what troubled me so. We found a fire in the garbage bin in the garage on the ground floor. My parents had told us to tell the neighbors in case of any problem so they came and helped squelch the fire and called my parents. The fact that I prevented what could have been a major fire was never spoken of later and seemingly forgotten, but I realized later that my brother and I may have been seriously injured during our sleep that night if I had not woken up due to my sensitivity. Autistic sensitivities can be useful sometimes!

My brother once tore the skin on his lower back while playing on rusty playground equipment. The sight of his gushing blood spooked me, but since we were alone I realized that I had to help him, nobody else would. I supported his limping body while we walked to the nearby hospital. Being alone was the key to this behavior, and without it I may have never exhibited the empathy that "saved" my mother from believing I just did not care about anyone else. Later, my mother often told me how this story happily affected her; from then on she unshakably believed I was very strong.

Once a year the Catholic Church of the town put together an overnight trip for the children of the parish, in which my brother and I participated. Thirty or so of us walked several hours to get to an unoccupied old abbey, in a natural and quiet environment. In order to distract ourselves on the way there, we sang endlessly. Every year, another little girl purposefully gave me "flats" (she stepped on my shoes' heels). She did it on purpose to tease me and this knowledge burnt but I did not even realize that maybe I could have said something to the priest who accompanied us. Once we reached our destination, my sleep was really troubled, what with this form of bullying and all the stress from sleeping and eating in close quarters with others.

Yet another day, I was visiting my mother at her work when one of the priests of the Catholic Church my mother worked with, said to me: "You are beautiful when you smile; too bad it is so rare." A compliment was rare, and I treasured it. I spent hours in front of the mirror practicing how to smile and from then on I became intent on smiling, even if many times it was just the muscles of my mouth that I curled upwards.

In Saint Pierre's church, I often went alone up the belfry, careful not to be on its stairs when the bells rang. The key to the belfry was hanging in my mother's office and I often took it without her knowledge, or so I like to believe. The climb up the narrow, dark and non-maintained stairs was difficult. The first time the huge bells started very near me I was paralyzed and covered my ears with my hands, I thought I was about to become deaf. But the result was worth it: a small space above the strife and noise of the world below, alone at last.

After school I was busy with many extra-curricular activities that channeled what would today have been called hyperactivity. My mother must instinctively have understood that I was doing better if I was constantly busy and in an environment providing an outlet to unwind after the enforced stillness of school.

I was getting good in tennis, and in my hometown I gained some respect that way. While it lasted it gave me a chance to be exposed to a wider area and experience a variety of social interactions. On the court I enjoyed figuring out strategies and I had a fascination with the court's lines. I often walked balancing on them for the longest I could. I wondered why the lines were here and not one inch further. It was all so arbitrary and a tiny little change could make the outcome different. I realized then that limits are just another man-made code, absurd at times. As soon as I hit a few rallies with another person, the little robot in my head started scheming: What was my opponent's weakest shot? Was the person left of right handed? Did she (or he, less often) run well? Was she a net or a base player?

My brother, Marie and I took gymnastic classes together. A few times a year, all the girls went by bus to nearby towns in order to compete, girls and boys separately. In the bus driving us to and from, the girls sang all together and I was thrilled to be for a short while integrated and part of a group.

Once a year our town gymnastic club put on a show on for parents. While I waited for my turn, which was a long time since my brother also was on the show and boys went first, I sat shivering on the cold bench next to my parents, my nervousness reached carefully hidden and untold paroxysms which affected my performance.

I especially liked the challenge of the balance beam and the uneven parallel bars which I was able to master with much hard practice. One time during a competition I was really nervous as judges observed my routine on the uneven parallel bars; despite the chalk I had put on beforehand the fleshy and callous part on the palms of my right hand suddenly ripped and blood trickled down on the bars. I finished my warm up routine feeling the pain and the blood on my hand and, after a few minutes rest and a bandage on, went right back to the uneven parallel bars; I was not about to let down my team. This time around the skin of my other hand also tore, but at least it did not bleed. For the next few weeks I wore bothersome bandages and could not close my fists.

Music was another extra-curricular activity we children did. In a children's music class, Marie and I learned to play the recorder, which we would later play in church at Christmas time with a third child. I still remember the difficult high note in the song for which I practiced, alone, again and again. When we were older Marie and I joined the adult choir that my mother and aunt sang in. The study of music theory was required for playing an instrument, and no matter how many years I studied it, I did not understand it. I was always surprised to be allowed to go on to the next level, which I believe happened mostly because I shamelessly copied from my classmates during the exams. At home we had an upright piano, but though I loved playing it, I was not very good. When I started to take piano lessons, my teacher was blind. I wondered how he could recognize the person who approached him, something which I later would myself be able to do (though I doubt it is comparable) during my illness in my mid-forties, when my sensitivities (including sounds) were the most acute.

The ballet classes I attended once a week took place in a building down the street from my home and I soon became totally engrossed with it. Alone at home I sometimes spent an entire afternoon practicing in our big upstairs room. I brought the living room record player upstairs and played classical airs such as "The Blue Danube" and Vivaldi's "The Four Seasons." Some of the muscles on my feet became so strong that I was able to stand on the tip of my toes without shoes on. I had dreams of becoming a skilled dancer, but I was too awkward with others. In fact the way in which I was made to stop was fishy. I did not want to stop and I think my mother was asked to stop taking me there due to my awkwardness with the other children.

My mother had played much volleyball in her youth and she wanted me to also play. For a few months I practiced with a volleyball team in an after school program. But after a few competitive games, the coach asked my mother that I stop, I never knew why exactly. Was it in order to console me that I was told I was too young and that I could do it again in a few years? Naturally I believed it, but it never happened. But a few years later I did play competitively again on the beach with my boyfriend. This occasioned for social awkwardness when I was left waiting forever on the sidelines to be invited to play in a game, when I was no longer dating my boyfriend. In hindsight I realized that this (and the same with ballet) probably had to do with my inability to socially function in a team.

Reading was another passion I threw myself into completely. Our house was on one end of a long street and at the other end—after a fifteen minute bike ride—there was a public library. Reading was a way to evade daily challenges and a strategy to make sense of the world. A book does not change, the printed characters always remain the same and at least you are alone while reading. I enjoyed the ink smell and I often sniffed the books up and down. I did not always understand what I read and I skipped many passages that seemed to me superfluous, for example introductions or prologues. I identified with the emotions in them and often cried when the characters hurt. One of my first lessons in willpower was when I had to stop myself from reading at night. My parents were happy that I read so much, except when I was so engrossed in a book that I read it late into the night or brought it to the dinner table and set it on my lap to keep reading while eating.

My parents were baffled by me: on one side I seemed to excel but on another side I failed. It seems often assumed that obsessive and repeated behaviors in autism are frightening and ought to be stamped out at all cost. To me these are simply a different way of being passionate and intensely focused. Most often, when nothing drives the passions to become unhealthy, if they are safe and not "evil" they most likely will fade out by themselves. It seems important to not attempt to stamp them out.

CHAPTER 4: A NEW HOME FOR A DIVIDED FAMILY

When I was ten or eleven, we moved to another part of Les Sables d'Olonne, in what would be my home for the rest of my years in France. My parents had always rented but this time they were able to borrow money to buy the house that had been my maternal grandparents' home, though it had to be entirely rebuilt because the walls were infested with termites. My father was the interior designer, which made for some odd but beautiful (to me) patterns, like the headboard in the shape of a half sun and painted orange that he built in his and my mother's bedroom, or the boldly striped wallpaper.

For autistic me, this new home was a boon. My brother and I each had our own bedroom on the second and last floor. This second floor would become the children's territory, as my parents' bed and bathrooms were downstairs and they only came up sporadically. We were given the choice of the color in which to paint our rooms and mine was blue. A year later I decided to peel the paint off my armoire and give it back its wood color by staining it with walnut stain. My parents thought this was an impossible task for such a young child, but once I had set my mind on something, just like many autistic people, I was extremely determined. To my parents' surprise, I accomplished the feat. My armoire looked much better, but it was really beyond my determination to do the same thing for the other pieces of furniture in my room, as I had secretly intended and they remained blue.

The electric radiator in my bedroom let out a strong burning dust smell when it had not been used for a while, a smell I could not stand. In the winter, in order to avoid it I did not want to let the radiator go unused for very long. So as soon as I entered my bedroom after a day at school, I turned it on regardless of the room's temperature. My mother thought it useless and costly. But I did not know how to explain myself, that it had nothing to do with the heat, and I knew she would not believe the extent of my sensory sensitivity, so I never told her the real reason behind my behavior.

On the same floor as the children's bedroom, there was a small bathroom without a toilet. However it had a bidet, and my brother and I often urinated in it since the toilet was far away downstairs. It angered my mother so much she eventually showed us the sponge and cleaning agent she had put in the closet and demanded that we clean after ourselves each time. I dutifully did this during daytime, even though I don't believe my brother did and I was often blamed by my mother for his transgressions.

In France the toilet is often a separate room, and ours was downstairs, a small dark place under the stairs and a daunting trip to accomplish in the dark of the night. My tummy often hurt with gastrointestinal pain and I was often very constipated. Sometimes I did not having a bowel movement for several days, once up to fifteen days, at which point my mother worried. Also, I was unable to have a bowel movement in strangers' homes.

Across from the children's bedroom there was a large guest bedroom, the "*grande chambre*," which when unoccupied (most of the time) became a play room. This bedroom was a space for make-believe adventures and an opportunity to develop useful skills on my own terms. It was the room where my brother and my girlfriend Marie were the actors made to abide to my directions in our little plays and other games. It was also the room where my brother and I played with the wonderful gifts my sister made a point to send us at Christmas and birthday times. As my sister earned her living creating art projects, like the candle-making kit or the pottery wheel, they often were of a craft-and-art type.

In each of the upstairs rooms, the slanted roof created eaves with many small closets, some with enough empty space for me to be able to crawl in, hide and rock. In *la grande chambre*, each of the closets contained treasures, one contained the paintings from my great grandfather, the second closet contained the glittery tiara and other beautiful clothes from my father's Russian first wife, which were a heaven for dressing up and pretend. The third closet on the other side of the room required a key (hidden in my parents' office downstairs) because it was the access to the roof insulation and fiber glass. I was very careful not to touch it, but my parents were quite upset the one time they found me there and after this they made sure to keep the key away.

Just like I had done in the previous house we lived in, with my brother's help I set up refuge in a part of the house where nobody else went: the loft over the garage could be climbed into thanks to a ladder. It was yet another dark and cold place where I could go and be left alone. This is not to be confused – it often seems to be in regard to autistic people- with being lonely, which is an emotion that I did not like at all.

As I have noted, the discord between my mother and I started early on, but as time passed it got worse. Some of my mother's family added more stress to this discord: they thought I was my father's daughter and they seemed to have feared that we were both somehow bad, while they favored my brother.

Tatie Sylvie, the aunt with whom I did many activities, was an exception to this as she came to have lunch with us every Sunday and often took me with in her little trips (for example when we visited several French castles). She also sewed and knit many clothes for my brother and me, and when my hair was longer she tightly braided it. Until my maternal grandmother *Mémé* died, when I was about twelve, Sylvie lived with her. I was never very close to *Mémé* and do not remember having much interactions with her. She hardly ever came inside our house, though my brother, my mother and I (not my father) often went to hers to watch television. Sylvie stayed alone in the same small house after her death.

When I was ten or so my parents kept asking that I stop shuffling my feet. But at times, and especially when I did not want to go someplace, my feet seem to stick to the floor as if I were dragging the weight of the world. I noticed that the slow and apathetic children were more likely to have an odd gait and I wanted to look like an athlete. So I carefully studied the way running with shuffling feet was done, with the soles flat and spread out, and the way the heels rather than the toes were set on bicycle pedals, and I consciously practiced to do just the opposite. It must have worked because my parents never told me again about my odd gait, though my brother often teased me about it, even when we were adults. When I was later aware of my autism and its connection to the pain in my left side, I realized that the strange gait of autistic individuals in childhood that often disappears as the child grows older, may in fact not really be gone, and instead the body posture may subtly become torqued.

The clothes I was wearing were another contention bone between my mother and me. My mother wanted me to wear skirts and dressed blouses and I wanted to wear baggy cotton instead of scratchy tight materials. My favorite sweaters, knitted by my aunt Sylvie (the seamstress), were big and made of cotton. When my mother bought store-made clothes, the labels painfully irritated my skin.

In elementary school I did not have to choose my clothes since I always had to wear the same smock—the one my aunt had made. But when I started middle school in a public school, choosing which clothes to wear proved too stressful to do in the morning rush, so I set out the clothes I would wear the next day the evening before, which worked well.

As a teenager, my unkempt hairdo and long bangs—a protective screen—was another area of contention between my mother and me. I did not like to look directly at people's face, and I did not want to do onto others what I found so unpleasant, looking at them in order to judge based upon appearances.

The tenser I became the more likely I was to react to touch, and many times my mother, who was the one most likely to experience this, told me how distressed she was then. She wondered if I really loved her. The experience of having an autistic child jerk away from a parent's touch is nothing personal; however as a mother I can understand the awful feeling of rejection.

Mealtimes at homes were sometimes becoming shouting matches as I refused to eat this or that. On the rare occasions we ate meat and there were tiny veins in it, I'd cut carefully around the veins. My frustrated parents tried to pry me into eating the food on my plate, sometimes serving it over the next day so that I'd finish it, which has been a way to successfully achieve forever distaste for that food. My mother often ended up cooking again and again simple dishes I liked, despite their lack of nutritive value, for example fries and waffles.

My relationship with my brother was also not so easy. Because I had to follow him a lot, I was exposed to diverse experiences, something I am grateful for. But it must have been difficult for my brother to drag his odd sister around, and he often mercilessly teased me. We did not have a television set but my aunt Sylvie, across the street from us, had one. After a late movie at her place my brother and I had to cross the street late at night in order to get to our house. I was easily upset and often moved to tears for this or for that bit of emotional scenery and my brother used the opportunity to scare me out of my wits. To his delight, frightened again, I often cried.

My brother was becoming quite skilled as a skier, so my parents sent us with a group to a ski resort. When my brother and I were about to vacate the chairlift at the summit leading to a black diamond trail, hoping to tease me he showed me the cross at the bottom of the cliff where someone had fallen from one of the chairs. After this scare, skiing down the steep path after him further paralyzed me. When I became stiff with cold I took my skis off and hiked my way down on foot.

My brother and I often practiced tennis together and when it was just the two of us the desire for competition wrecked the fun. My brother would often play foul just so he could win. I so easily fell for it that to my frustration he often ended up winning.

An uncle gave my brother a job in his bakery starting when my brother was about twelve. I was jealous of my brother's earnings. At Christmas, a few months after I had been caught stealing candy in his store, this uncle gave my brother a shiny red bicycle and only a small bag of chocolate candy to me. It stung.

My father did not like television but my mother, my aunt and I regularly watched a show called *Des Chiffres et des Lettres*, or *Of Numbers and of Letters*. I was fascinated by the letter part in which the show's two guests had to come up with the largest word with the letters they had been given, and this within a limited amount of time. I was quite good at this and often came up with a word before my aunt and my mother. In the same vein, I excelled at the game of Scrabble, a game my mother agreed to play with my aunt and me.

Bitterly I found out over and over that my mother and I did not understand one another. She was usually the main person to bear the effects of my discomfort and tantrums. When I became a teenager I blamed her for my misery and screamed it to all who would offer a sympathetic ear. She may have dismissed and misunderstood my autistic challenges, but at least she did not to drag me in situations that would surely have cognitively destroyed me, like bringing me to see plenty of doctors or putting me away in institutions. Neither of my parents were "helicopter parents" and they often let me be. I do not know how to say how important this was to my development—and by what I hear, the same is probably true for many autistic children.

CHAPTER 5: A MIDDLE SCHOOL NEAR THE ATLANTIC OCEAN

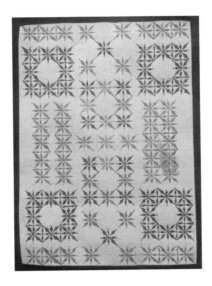

Repetitive stim pattern, circa 1972

When I started to go to a public middle school (which was on the same campus as the high school), I experienced an expanding awareness of my different ways. Many of my dreams were dashed. Others also started to notice I did not fit so well and my struggles showed more clearly. The first year Marie and I were in the same class and it helped. We usually biked together to and from school, meeting every day at a designated spot where our routes met.

Academically I was an average student. In foreign languages if I was able to hear and speak the languages in a real context I had a much better chance to make sense of them. For example I became quite skilled in English as I practiced it with several tennis players from other countries when they stayed at our place. Also, I went to England twice (once as an exchange student and once as a failed au-pair). German was another matter. In class I was bored by the teacher and I doodled repeatedly on the blank pages of my notebooks a peculiar pattern doodle. This doodle was another type of autistic stim, and as an adult I still can draw it from memory. I built the pattern based on the lines (which, like the tennis court lines, I obsessed over) of my notebook: French notebook lines have both horizontal and vertical ruling. I felt this doodle to be such an intimate example of my autism that I appended a single one at the end of each chapter of this book and I use it as my banner on my blog, Autizen.com.

I may have been able to keep up a discussion with adults but underneath there was a problem with the child who in many situations could not do very well with her peers. My teachers wondered if the age discrepancy between me and my fellow students was the reason for my challenges and they had me stay back one year, which meant I was now the same age as my classmates.

For a few months I imagined that I had special powers and acted with my peers as if I could tell their future. I told them that a little green jade stone I called Nabuchodonosor gave me supernatural powers. I put the stone in the other child's hands and made up stories that made them happy, like the number of children a girl would have, the type of person they would fall in love with, what would be their future profession, etc. I was amazed by the credulity of my listeners and I realized then that since it was so easy for people to make up tales, I'd better be weary of the tales I was myself bound to be told at times.

Once I had a fistfight with Bruno in the school's yard. A few months later, Bruno ganged up with Luc (we were on the same tennis team) and another boy and the three of them threw bits of foxtails at me in order to taunt me. I was paralyzed with fear and unable to move. One foxtail crawled up so near my throat and mouth that I became obsessed with the thought that I would swallow it.

The cafeteria lunch took up thirty minutes during which I usually obsessed about food and contamination. I believed that only packaged food that had not been touched was safe. Thus in the school's cafeteria I only ate the food that was served wrapped, mainly the crackers and yogurts, and this left me hungry.

Maybe to make up for this, on my way to and from school every day I stopped at a candy store and bought a lot of candy. Eventually I became addicted to sugar and on top of the candy stores I often biked every day to several pastry shops in order to buy two or three pastries at a time. Naturally the change money my parents gave me every month was not enough to sustain this habit, so I stole coins from my mom's purse despite her anger when she happened to notice it.

The school's midday break lasted two hours. This meant that after lunch in the cafeteria I had ninety minutes of unstructured time before resuming classes. It deeply hurt that I was not accepted in the little groups of students that were scattered on the grounds, with Marie in one of them. At first I huddled in hidden places to read but eventually I developed another obsession: I kicked a pebble over and over around the yard. I tried to keep the same pebble day after day, noticing where I left it at the end of the lunch break so I could use it again the next day. I counted how much the pebble traveled, wondering if it had made it to China yet. Would I ever be able to travel thus?

It is no surprise then that the school requested I no longer eat lunch at the school's cafeteria. Instead I went home and my brother followed. As was the custom in France my mother also had a long lunch break during which she had barely enough time to come home and cook. It may have been an added responsibility for my mother as it increased her already full load but to her credit she never made me feel guilty. At home during lunch my father, my mother, my brother and I were now together, which I liked much better than the school's cafeteria. The problem with a child not being given reasons for changes like this is that then she may think it is her fault, as I did.

I took much pain to hide my different perceptions and the ensuing behaviors. Not being diagnosed autistic as a child was my saving grace. Had I been dragged to doctors, I may have been labeled and looked down at. An autistic diagnostic label can be cause for troubles, and especially at that time in France. Many teachers and other support staff feel superior to their diagnosed charge and opportunities are denied, which can be perceived so overwhelming by an autistic person that we may fall into the abysses leading to mental illnesses, medical drugs, institutions, or suicide and other problems. When autism is thought to be a disease that must be cured, the fragile and nervous child might be destroyed by inappropriate treatments. We are often so sensitive it is as if we had an insincerity meter, and the smugness of the people around us (who are often completely unconscious of it) may seriously rock us. On the other hand I have now met many younger autistic people for whom being diagnosed autistic has had several positive effects on the individual. As a teacher friend told me, "How can I help if I do not know the child has a challenge?" Allowing access to the now much improved services can obviously be very helpful, the answer to the situation is not simple at all, autism has many facets and I certainly do not have all the answers.

The Atlantic Ocean which borders les Sables d'Olonne made for many interesting experiences; it was a natural environment that allowed me to indulge in some of my autistic wandering ways. Often I took off and disappeared for a little while. *La Plus Belle Plage d'Europe* (the most beautiful beach in Europe) was the cute and arguable nickname given to the large beach of the town, a stretch of fine yellow sand with a gentle grade. It would later be spoiled by disasters like the Amoco Cadiz oil tanker spill.

At low tide the sea recessed far and I could then see for myself that there was no rock and not much seaweed either. Consequently when the tide covered the beach I was able to swim without fear of the unseen bottom. After a big storm there may be patches of seaweed in the ocean, but since I was now older I was able to brace myself to walk around it knowing that a few feet further water would be clear.

After I had mastered enough of a mix of dog-paddling and breast stroke I was able to swim alone and I enjoyed the waves which enveloped me in their cold and short-lived embraces. I devised a game to not be thrown backward by a big wave, diving instead to the bottom and swimming against the wave's current. I sometimes ended up a few feet ahead and I loved the feeling of the strong push against my body in the dark and quiet underwater while I disliked the blinding light that met me when I came up to the surface to check my advance and breath.

Each summer day a lifeguard put up a flag of different color to warn the people about the state of the sea: green for calm, orange for stormy and red to forbid any swim. Orange was my favorite color because then there were less people and the waves were more challenging, giving the possibility of exhilarating strong embraces. Still I was careful in this type of weather to not go so far that I was unable to touch ground.

I liked the beach most either early or later at dusk when it was quite empty of people. Once while swimming alone at dusk and staying not too far from the cost, a slimy cold thing brushed against my right thigh. I was so scared I swam out of the water with all the speed I could muster and I never went swimming alone in the dark again. Windsurfing and surfing were trendy sports in our seaside little town and my brother and I had both types of boards in our garage. Some young people were very good at it and cliques of young teenagers formed around the few extremely skilled ones. I badly wanted to be part of those cliques, but though I knew everyone, and I sometimes attempted to wait with the other girls on the beach for the guys' return, I always felt like an outsider. I consoled myself by reflecting on how silly the "waiting girls" were.

In the winter, once the summer crowds were gone, the beach was often deserted. Many of Les Sables d'Olonne inhabitants hardly went to the beach. When the weather was so stormy that nobody was on the beach, I sometimes hiked the length of the beach and took my shoes and socks off to wade in the icy water. My goal was to walk to the smaller of the two piers that marked the entrance to the harbor. Once there, I sat behind the light house and remained alone there for long periods of times, tucked away and invisible to all but the waves that crashed below me, breathing in the strong sea breeze.

At other times I went to jog on the beach early in the morning. I was jogging in the less crowded woods that line the coast on the northern part of les Sables d'Olonne when I had a scary encounter. Wild boars migrate through these woods every year and I met a lonely one. I jumped on the nearest tree and from the safety of that perch I observed that after just a few long minutes the boar cantered away. But I was so frightened I remained a long time in the tree. Once I finally climbed down I ran to my bike, which was parked near the road half a mile away. I figured that it would be safe where the noise of the traffic would keep away the boars.

Unaware, I sometimes wandered away from inhabited places in order to find a spot where I could be alone and without the uncomfortable stress of social behavior. Once I became stuck for several hours on a rock as the upward tide encircled it. My mother was frantic with worry when she finally found me.

I also enjoyed hiding away inside German bunkers that were placed at strategic points on the coast near les Sables d'Olonne and eventually I knew most of them in the biking perimeter of our small town. I usually biked to the same spot on the beach and parked my bike near its entrance. People often seemed to have "their spot" on the beach as I knew it, and we often found each other and greeted one another that way.

One day as I was returning, I walked barefoot up the ramp to get to my bike and I tripped on an uneven stone. The nail of one of my toes tore off and only one corner of it stayed attached to my skin. Foolishly refusing the help that was offered several times, I limped in pain during the five- or six-block walk to the hospital. There I learned that this was a common injury with fishermen and the doctor knew exactly how to sew the nail back on to allow for the new one to grow back straight underneath.

When I knew that the beach would be mostly empty, I sometimes took the family dog for walks. On the way to the beach and as I rode my bike he led the way, but on the way back I am ashamed to remember that I sometimes dragged him along.

I do not remember my mother once forbidding me to wander around and it probably would not have been worth the battle. I suspect that the times and the environment then were safer and my mother did not need to worry too much unless my absence was too long, in time I always came back home. I believe that many autistic children ought to be given more leeway and trust if at all possible.

CHAPTER 6: I HAVE FRIENDS
BUT I AM DEPRESSED

Like many autistic children I was more comfortable with older people since with them I could speak at length about whatever interest sparked my passion. Caroline and Paul were a married couple, Parisian friends of my parents who often stayed with us during the summers. My brother and I called them aunt and uncle. Despite the fact that Caroline and Paul belonged to a fancy bridge club in Paris and were more skilled than my parents, the four of them often played bridge late in the night, sometimes with much arguing.

Caroline and Paul were heavy smokers and the smell of their cigarettes is definitely one way I remember them. Another vivid memory is of the night when Paul or Caroline left the faucet in the upstairs bathroom slightly turned on and it dripped every few seconds. There was only one thin wall between the faucet and my bed and to my hypersensitive ears the sound of that drip grated so much on my nerves that, after turning in my bed restlessly for several hours, I finally had to idea to get up and go tie a towel around the faucet.

Paul and Caroline were one of the few remaining French hat makers and their dainty and quirky Parisian factory, full of wooden hat molds, was colorful. I visited it only once but it made a big impression on my perceptions: drawings (of hats of course), colors, glue smells, lights and strange mold shapes with or without hats on them. This business of theirs was quite famous in the Parisian fashion world.

Christine was another adult friend whom I had first met when my mother and she became friends, and I remained friend with her even when she no longer kept in touch with my mother. I often also saw her at choir and at church where she played the organ. When she became my high school physics-chemistry teacher, in order to escape home and find some solace and relief, almost every Sunday I biked over to her home to have lunch with her and her children. Christine was quite the cook and she always made these delicious desserts. Her delicious cooking introduced me to the tastefulness of vegetarian dishes, though she cooked vegan dishes on the side for herself: she had food allergies and her health was compromised. Christine is one of the few French people with whom I remain in contact to this day.

A Catholic priest with whom my mother worked, was especially supportive of me during my adolescence: about once a week I met with him in his office in one of the church's adjacent buildings in order to speak with him, a therapeutic moment I looked forward to. He often came to the beach with us and once he drove me and a teenage friend to a feminist concert. He also took tennis lessons with my father and he was very enthusiastic about it.

I was always exposed to many people, including other children, which was good for my social skills development. In a smaller town a few kilometers from us lived during the summers the D. family. The grandparents owned a beautiful eighteenth century large stone mansion. They too were avid bridge players and my parents often drove to their place, with Caroline and Paul at summertime. Sometimes they brought my brother and me along so we could play and spend the night with their three grandchildren. Together we had numerous children's adventures on the large property and its adjoining gardens or another nearby beach. Meal times there were complete with a dinner bell for the maid when needed, and we had to really watch our table manners (for example, we were made to pay one cent when we swore).

When I was a teenager, many friends eventually became upset with me and rejected me. I cannot pinpoint an exact moment in time when my brother and I drifted apart, but at some point he too started to spend all his time with his friends and did not want me to have any contact with him or them. Sometime during middle school, my girlfriend Marie became very upset with me and stopped being my friend. Suddenly one day she refused to speak with me and accused me of fibbing when I said I fainted because of the noise. When she stopped hanging with me she invoked an argument which involved other young teenagers. Later I thought she might have been spooked the time I masturbated in front of her under the tennis club bleachers; I masturbated a lot in public these days. Since we had been such close friends, Marie's decision brought me much misery and felt like a great tragedy to me. I had absolutely no idea what she exactly reproached me with and for many years afterward I was sore.

But since I could not figure out what I had done wrong, I blamed the others, a habit that many of us, whether autistic or not, are ingrained with. At that time I started to be so afraid of offending unintentionally that I abided by manners most people forget as soon as they learn them. In social environments, I covered up my deep discomfort by rattling off incessantly and when with my family I often stayed away in my bedroom.

Sometimes when I spoke, it was so full of impreciseness, or was monosyllabic, that it resulted in much misunderstanding without me being aware of it. For example, I was often imprecise and used the word "thing" a lot (I still do this presently in the English language). There are many words for "the thing" in French: *le truc* or *le bidule* or *le machin*.

There were many other short-lived friendships, the ones I mentioned here were the ones that so impacted me that I still remember it. It never crossed my mind that I had different challenges, and nobody around me figured it either; autism was just not as much on the radar. Nowadays, I probably would be labeled in one way or another, maybe improperly.

As my differences showed more and more I became more depressed. Whatever grief took place in a specific moment, it only added to an already present bottomless sadness. The terrible and wrenching pains I often experienced in silence often did not show and I was not aware that it was different. I thought everyone was like me. I cried a lot and I became skilled at doing it without any conspicuous sniffling that would have given me out and provoked questions I could not have answered. I found out that if I resisted the urge to wipe away my tears, once they had dried no trace of them would remain.

I was about twelve the first time I ran away after an argument with my father. I biked half way down the rainy street when I realized I had nowhere to go. I fought my impulses back, let go of injured pride and returned. I believed that my father's behavior had been unjust, but for the sake of peace I figured I'd better let him think as he wished. My father's intuitive reaction was helpful, he did not say a word nor show any facial expression when he saw me come back. It was a lesson that helped me to endure many future impulsive moments.

On a long drive home back from a tennis tournament while I sat in the backseat of someone else's car, my jaw locked completely shut and I was unable to open my mouth for a few pain-filled and anxious hours. It was just after a few days of immense stress in a dormitory with the other children teasing me and I had not slept a wink, I was exhausted. Since no one in the car noticed that I was not speaking, and once the lockjaw released I did not know how to put into words what had just happened, I never told anyone about this terrifying moment.

It was a hot summer day when, with the vague hopes to reach a city and find somewhere else to live, I ran away on my bike. After several kilometers under a scorching sun I was so thirsty I stole a glass bottle of pop that was sold at a country fair I biked by. I cut myself when trying to open it with a rock and the sight of blood brought me back to reality: I realized it was naïve of me to believe I could achieve independence this way. I found shelter in a farm and asked its owners if I could place a phone call to my parents. The kind woman took me with her to help in the field and we picked tomatoes while I was waiting for my cousins to pick me up. This activity was a solace in my distressed state.

Wishing to leave home, for two weeks I stayed at *l'aumonerie*, the Catholic youth center that the priest I liked led. After two weeks I became lonely for home and tired of a diet consisting of tea and bread. This taught me a useful lesson about the importance of reality and the comforts of home.

Thoughts of ending my life started to churn in my head and each time I rode through an intersection I knew to be dangerous, I rode at full speed without looking left or right: maybe if I rode my bike recklessly enough a car would hit me and I would be able to put an end to my misery. When I realized that an accident at the speed I could afford on my old bike was more likely to leave me injured and paralyzed than dead, I stopped. Another attempt to kill myself was the time I swam away far at sea. I naively hoped that I would become so exhausted that I would drown. When faced with reality, and the cold water, I realized that drowning of exhaustion would be a long affair. And so I asked a nearby boat to take me back to shore, where I found my mother waiting unhappily. I pretended to be angry with her but her presence comforted me.

I did not know how to explain all this and I did not speak about my challenges, which fooled people into believing nothing important was the matter. It was really fortunate for me that my nervous system was young and my environment was somewhat stable and safe, I was somehow able to pretend to be "normal." Nervousness caused me to become like an extremely taut rubber band, ready to snap at what appeared to others to be the lightest of provocation—they were not small to me.

CHAPTER 7: TENNIS SCENE, HIGH SCHOOL AND TURMOIL

Playing tennis, circa 1977

Once I started to play competitively, my father invested much time in registering and driving me to tennis tournaments, especially when school was off in the summers.

Whacking the ball was a healthy way to release some of my anger. But I did not like the competitive part and it felt absurd to want to defeat someone who was just like me and wanted to win. Sometimes I would enter a tournament only to find myself competing for the second time in a few months against my friend Melanie! A young tennis player taught me a lesson about the power of focus. We were competing against one another when during a tense point she did not notice a ball that came rolling from another court onto the middle of ours. I, on the other hand, was easily distracted and completely lost my focus. Sometimes during a competitive point I would see the leaf that fell off a nearby tree or the rabbit that ran across the lawn just behind the court. But I had to realize that if I wanted to win, in whichever environment, I could not afford to watch and think about the nearby falling leaf at the ends of its life, and so I worked hard to focus as much as I could.

The following recounts the most memorable tennis match I ever played, about one driving hour away from my hometown. My mother rounded a few of our teenage friends to come and watch and there was a small monetary price to be won. Because that day's match was the women's final, it took place on a Sunday, when more people could come and watch. I knew it was possible to win because I had beaten my opponent a year earlier and she was a middle-aged player, which meant there was much less possibility of a drastic level improvement.

I woke up that Sunday morning with much anxiety. To keep stress to a minimum, I stuck to the usual routine. I packed early on the beloved blue bag, the one that had a new zipper my aunt had taken the trouble to sew on (my son would use it years later). I took much care about my clothes; I wore my favorite white tennis outfit underneath my warm up suit. I so wanted to have a sponsor like some players I knew who knew better how to hustle. In order to protect my feet I put on two pairs of socks and I made sure my toe nails were cut short. I repeated to myself what I had learned in previous competition: that whatever would be, would be.

That day was one of those beautiful spring days and the match started on time. There were none of the delays that sometimes happened, mostly because it rained and matches had to be rescheduled at a later time. When this happened the added waiting time often led me to sink further into a nervous state. After the few starting minutes during which the usual stomach knots prevented my moving around properly, I loosened up and started to hit the solid ground strokes that were my trademark.

At one point during the match a call was disputed: had the ball landed right on the line or just outside? The decision would result in a clear gap in the score. In this case, the surface on which we played was red clay and the mark the ball had left was visible enough for the call to be correctly made. It was in my favor and after this, the gap between us widened further and further.

I won the match in a rather prompt manner, a good thing because I never did well with lengthy matches. The longer a match lasted the less I was able to stay focused and my back tired quickly. With the money I earned that day I bought the jean jacket that is presently hanging on the tree rack behind me. The small towel I also won that day would become a mascot. Because I have kept them into middle age, these and the blue bag became the objects of much sentimental attachment.

Since the town was a summer resort, my hometown tennis club had its two annual tournaments during the summer, when the beach attracted many. These tournaments were part of the European tour where international high-ranked players could earn money. In exchange for their participation they were fed and lodged during the tournament. Thus for a few years my parents hosted foreign players for a few days every July and August. Some players came as far as South and North America. As a competitive tennis player myself, I was the one in our family with whom the foreigners interacted most and this allowed me to hone my tennis skills; I sometimes practiced with players of an excellent level. Naturally I also often introduced them to the beach. English was often the only language we were able to communicate in, and in this way I practiced speaking English in a real way outside of school. The improvement of my language skill in English showed on my school's results in this area, and this also helped me take the bold decision to move and emigrate to the United States a few years later.

Thanks to tennis I was respected and had friends. Most important to me was the adult team I started to play with when I was sixteen. The fact that I was one of the better tennis players on the team helped me to feel wanted and accepted. In the end, though tennis was good for me in many practical ways, tournament play with its social and sensory demands was more than I could sustain and I suddenly and inexplicably lost all my energy. I was about seventeen when I lost all strength on the tennis court. Practice times that I had previously enjoyed became grueling, having to pick up balls and the drills exhausted me. I started to lose all the time and my ranking went down. My disappointed father took me to meet Henri Cochet, one of legendary four musketeers who was training future tennis stars in Paris and was a former friend of my father. I knew it was hopeless, I did not have it anymore in me, but I did not know how to explain this. This trip was awful; during it I was completely silent and upset. By the time I got to see Henri Cochet I was just unable to say anything and my performance on the court was also impaired.

Because I had stayed back a year earlier on, in high school I was the same age as my peers. Marie no longer spoke with me and my brother was a boarder at another school. Every morning before the first bell rang, in yet another attempt to fit in I greeted five or six other young student ladies according to the French custom, which is to kiss lightly two times on each cheek. With my sensory challenge to touch this felt like if I was going through the gauntlet.

My grades where often either high or low, and the papers I wrote were often thought to be either brilliant or obscure. Mathematics, physics and scientific subjects were confusing; I did not always understand their connection with reality. I had a strange logic and processed problems in a different way that often took longer, though I sometimes manage to resolve it anyway. More often than not, I was unable to do what was asked. My teacher in *physique-chimie*, Christine, was a friend and sometimes tutored me.

I still read voraciously. Now a teenager, I read a book called "*une abeille contre la vitre*," "a bee against the window," (it is not translated in English), by Gilbert Cesbron. The book made much of an impact on me. In it a young woman tries to kill herself because her face is ugly. I could empathize with wanting to die, with being different and feeling like an outsider.

The difference with the book was that I wanted to change my brain, not my face. I believed (rightly so as it turned out many years later) my brain was the main reason behind my different ways.

At the end of the school day I sometimes walked by the cafés where young people my age were hanging out. I always hoped to be invited inside and I asked myself over and over what I had done that they would not do so. The few times I found an excuse to be inside with them I was overwhelmed—there was much smoking—and I spoke incessantly and as if I knew everything. At this time in my life I dearly struggled to master the French saying *"le silence est d'or et la parole est d'argent"* (silence is gold and word is silver). In the cafés I was upset by the din and the smoke of cigarettes. The one time I tried smoking like the others I choked and felt poisoned.

When I was about sixteen I started to have seizures every few weeks or so. At first they lasted barely a few seconds and I could hide them. When asked why I fainted I said it was because of the noise, but this was ignored and I was thought to be crazy. When I once passed out in the living room, my parents were just on the other side of the room having tea. They believed I was only seeking their attention and they remained in their seats drinking their tea. After a few minutes (or was it seconds?), I woke up with a cold floor under me. When I realized my parents were not going to help I managed to stand up and went to cry myself to bed, feeling utterly abandoned and having lost all hope in my parents. I learned that day that one should never ignore distress signals in another, no matter how they do not make sense.

When my brother was home, we fought constantly. When he provoked my anger my strength was tenfold. Once when he locked himself in his bedroom to get away from me, I kicked the door so violently I made a dent in it; years later it is still there, covered by white tape. These fights stopped abruptly the fateful day when he punched me and I became nauseous. After that he severed all ties with me.

Hoping it would help, my parents let me stay at Christine's home for a few months. Her eldest son and I were one year apart in age and while I lived with them he introduced me to his favorite classical tunes during our afternoon teas. The music had quite an effect on me; it penetrated me to the marrow. Combined with a proper diet and supportive care, this allowed me to come back on track

When the results of the baccalaureate (the French high school exit examination) were posted for all to see, I was too limp with worry to fend off the crowd of students who were jostling to get to the posted results. My boyfriend's brother, Bernard was quite tall so he went to read them for me. Maybe because I still had enough self-confidence thanks to my parents' tenuous respect and tennis, I passed despite the low overall mention, "*passable*" or barely passing.

CHAPTER 8: I LEARN OF MY FATHER'S SECRET PAST AND I FALL APART

A few months before I graduated from high school, an older friend, introduced me to Alain. He was a few years older than me and a medical student in Paris. His parents had a vacation home in Les Sables d'Olonne. When I was getting ready for our first date at a dancing club, a terrible anxiety that was almost debilitating overcame me. A boyfriend might help me be seen and help me overcome my loneliness, I thought. What should I wear, what would he say, what would I do? I decided to wear my green and white ruffled skirt. Alain seemed to want the two of us to get together and I was happy to comply. Alain and I became a couple that evening and when college started at the end of a hectic summer, I went to an elite boarding school near Paris that was near him.

For a few months I was a full time boarder at an elite school in Versailles studying literature and philosophy. Several weekends, despite the rigorous schedule, I stayed with Alain at his parents' tiny apartment. This was hard on everyone and when I dropped out of that school and went to the University of Creteil, after a brief stint at the University of La Sorbonne, Alain's parents bought a one-bedroom apartment for us in a suburb of Paris near them. We lived there together for two years.

I went to a party in the home of one of my childhood friends. Parties made me ill but I did not pay attention to my unease. That night the loud music was deafening and the throbbing lights blinded me. Sebastien, whom I had a crush on, was engrossed with his new girlfriend and ignored me. I remained sad and aloof the entire time, feeling sick with unease and unable to mingle. I spent most of the time shivering alone outside.

The city environments did not agree with me and I fainted more often. Except for one instance when I bit my tongue at school, these seizures were "petit mal." They often happened while I was walking on a sidewalk, after a truck had gone by in a tumult of hissing sounds. Since I could usually tell when I was about to faint, I sat down wherever I was—once it was in the middle of the street I was crossing—and I warned the people around me to not worry, the spell would quickly pass. I'd forget to tell the bystanders that I'd probably be able to stand back up and leave unattended.

My mother took me to a renowned Parisian mental hospital to have a brain scan. This was about 1984 and in France, autism was deemed a mental retardation illness related to schizophrenia. If you were obviously not mentally retarded, it could not be autism. The doctor who scanned the results told me it was the strangest epilepsy he had ever seen and prescribed barbiturates. When I heard his findings I was alone with him. As usual, I was intimidated by his position of authority and too afraid to ask questions. I was relieved that no further medical testing was required; I found the process frightening. But I felt uselessly drugged by the barbiturates—once my father thought I was asleep on my bed, when in fact I could not move at all—and not much later I abruptly stopped taking them, without any worsening of my condition.

The next year I went to the University of Creteil, which was closer to where I lived than La Sorbonne. I could sometimes go there by bike rather than the horrible bus. My commute to the university took me past what was one of the largest roundabouts in France. Biking through it was dangerous and deafening as trucks and cars swirled around coming from all directions. At times I became so overwhelmed and disoriented, I could not remember the correct turn.

One month before my university end of the year exams, my mother came to see me in Paris with a specific agenda on her mind: to tell me some of my father's history, an untold secret that she felt entitled to tell me now that I was an adult. The secret was that in his early twenties my father had killed somebody and was sentenced to life imprisonment on Devil's Island, a notorious penal colony off the coast of South America, in French Guyana. My mother told me there was a book written about the place, *Papillon* by Henri Charriere. My older sister was born during my father's exile (with a native Indian mother). When my father returned to France, he recognized his daughter as his legitimate daughter and cared for her. My mother concluded proudly that few convicts showed such loyalty. When Charles de Gaulle became the president of France, he closed the penitentiary and my father was able to come back to France.

I read the book *Papillon* immediately and some of the descriptions in it chillingly reminded me of my father. Learning my father's story was a terrible shock. Suddenly I was the daughter of a murderer and convict. I was unable to study for my university exams and failed. Several weeks later I was back at my parents in les Sables d'Olonne for the summer.

I celebrated my twentieth birthday with drugs and booze at Alain's vacation home. Alain and I did not spend the night together; we'd had too many disagreements already. When I woke up with a terrible hangover the next day at my parent's home, I decided right there and then to end it all, my life was too painful and tiring and I tried to kill myself. This suicide attempt was way savvier than what I had tried earlier, as I swallowed half of the barbiturates pills in my possession. Because Alain was a medical student I had obtained more than the usual amount, a fact that, as an adult, strikes me as rather irresponsible (a young person might not be reliable with such dangerous drugs).

Fortunately for me, as I was swallowing the pills some kind of survival instinct took over, I envisioned myself paralyzed or brain dead, and I stopped. I called the younger doctor whom my family was seeing at the time. I had played tennis with him a few times and we had some of the same friends. This helped me be more comfortable around him. He asked me to make myself throw up but it was already too late for that (I tried) and he took me to the nearest clinic to have a stomach pump performed.

During the night, while I was half unconscious with drugs I fell off the bed and broke the intra-venous line in my arm. The sight of the blood startled me out of my drugged stupor and I rang the attendant on duty. When this older man found me lying on the floor half naked, he asked me if he could have sex with me, despite my semi-conscious state. Not having the energy to defend myself, I let him do it while I mumbled it was a way to atone for my father's crime.

The next day, as I was relaxing on the beach in the warm sand I told this to Alain. Our relationship was already rocky however at this point we were still a couple. Instinctively afraid of authorities, I asked him not to tell the police, but he disregarded my request. At the police station I was too nervous to say much and I could not describe the attendant so well. Often, my way to size a person up is to pick up on emotional clues; I don't recognize faces very well. Several weeks later I saw the guy in the police station. Despite not being sure of his face, my stomach acted up, my body was telling me this was the man. I did not feel empowered to press charges and so I rationalized my decision, thinking it was not up to me to wreck the lives of the man's five children. I did not press charges and I got the feeling that many in that little provincial town assumed I was guilty.

I ended my relationship with Alain, who was himself miserable at that time; his only brother, Bernard, had just died in a freak catamaran accident while crewing for Phillipe Jeantot, founder of the Vendee Globe round-the-world sailing race. A month after our break up, Alain came to my work in the Town Hall's Lost and Found Department. In front of everyone in the office, he went down on his knees and begged me to forgive him. But being in public most always makes my behavior worse. It is as if my nervous system becomes paralyzed; I am dumb and say or behave in stupid and mean ways. That day was no exception and I laughingly told Alain off. At the end of the day, when I was finally alone on my bike and found myself shocked by my earlier behavior I cried and screamed in the empty streets that lead me home, but it never occurred to me that I could call Alain and explain myself.

After this my life spun out of control for a year. I dropped out of school and I had sex with two older men. I wanted to achieve a semblance of self-esteem and I believed that if men slept with me it must mean that I was loved and lovable. Instead horrific things took place.

Less than two months after the break up with Alain, I met Yvon, the first of the two older men I made the mistake to sleep with. I met him through one of the priests my mother worked with, of all places! Yvon was visiting les Sables d'Olonne for a few days and we hit it off. A week later I decided to hitchhike to the town of Rouen where Yvon lived. My upset mother did not want me to go and would have nothing to do with it, so I swore I would not bother her with anything and I went anyway. Once I made it to Yvon's home in Rouen, after a night I have no memory of, at the breakfast table I was horrified to notice that my lover's daughter was only a year or two younger than me.

I immediately fled his home and went to hitch car rides back to my hometown. But I was deeply upset and in a sort of trance. As I stepped out of a car just on the outskirts of Rouen I slammed the car door shut on my thumb. The car started to move but the driver stopped when he heard me frantically pounding on the window with my other hand! I told him I was OK (I thought I was, I often make this mistake in the heat of the moment) and he left, but after a few steps I fainted on the side walk.

When I came to, I was surrounded by strange men in white robes. I did not know where I was, who was with me and my thumb throbbed. Pure fear struck me and I lost touch with reality, I fought these men with all my might until I lost consciousness. When I woke up in the city's hospital I realized that they had sedated me. The sedative I was given had the effect of giving me for a few hours after my awakening complete amnesia. The tree I could see through the window could have been on another planet. When asked, I could not remember my mother's name and anyway I did not want to since I had angrily told her she would not hear from me. I never had a chance to tell anyone that my thumb was the real problem.

Despite this, my mother was at my bedside a few hours later (I never knew how she had learned about my accident). She was angry that she had had to come and drive for several hours and I did not dare tell her about my thumb. We left the hospital together on rather cold terms. She used this visit as an opportunity to have dinner with friends of hers in Rouen. I did not want to be more of a nuisance for her and since nobody was asking me anything I still did not say a word about the pain in my thumb. It is only after about three hours of driving as we neared les Sables d'Olonne that I brought it up. My mother took me to our hometown's hospital, where my thumb was finally cared for and during a few weeks I wore a brace. Years later I realized that it could have been worse, that in my highly nervous state the sedative could have killed me.

I have several times read of instances when an autistic child's silence upon being gravely hurt is thought to mean that the child does not feel the hurt. Nothing is less true, I suspect it is just the opposite, the child feels it ten times more in his or her nerves and is overwhelmed by this. What happened for me that time in Rouen (and in many other milder instances), is that I blocked out the pain. I had learned to repress pain from birth and it had become such a second nature that I was disconnected from my feelings.

Jérome, the second older man I slept with a few months later, was the director of an adult camp for mentally disturbed people that my distraught mother thought might help. The camp took place in the vicinity of Jérome's house in the countryside. Due to scheduling reasons I stayed at his house a few days before the others arrived. The family, complete with wife and two young children, were *soixante-huitards*, or "sixty-eighters." This was the nickname given to French inhabitants who espoused the views of the French political upheaval of 1968 and embraced the "back to nature" movement of the time, akin to America's flower children. In Jérome's household, and in my eyes, it meant a lot of work for the mother as, for example, she had to wash the laundry by hand for a family of four. The night Jérome slept with me, I was too young to realize what I was doing to his marriage. I thought he loved me. I was not good at disguising the truth and when his wife found out she made sure we were never around one another again.

But a few months later, Jérome had another opportunity without his wife around and even though I did not want it to happen. I had previously told my mother about it and she had been so upset I understood I'd better not do this again. That time, many of the group's participants were meeting for one night in Paris and we all slept in our sleeping bags on the floor. When Jérome crept by mine I felt I had no choice but to let him in so as not to wake up the others. When I told my mother she put an immediate stop to it and I never had to go back to any such group.

These incidents left me with a sour taste in my mouth. At the time I was unaware of the trauma that would plague me for many years after; I did not clearly understand that the older men who had sex with me took advantage of my naivety. If these men were to stand in front of me now, chances are I would not recognize them. Around the same time, I also had two other one night stands with men of my generation. I still can't believe how I let myself be so easily encroached upon.

CHAPTER 9: PICKING MYSELF UP AND ATTENDING COLLEGE IN NANTES

Hitchhiking to Nantes - circa 1985

Forever trying to help me, my father sent me to visit my sister in Canada for several months. My mother was against this trip but it was a complete change of scenery that actually helped me in many ways. I had never seen that much snow and it was very cold in Montreal in the winter! My sister showed much support, as she has my entire life. She took me to see a doctor despite the fact that in order for her insurance to cover it, I had to swap identity with her (we had the same last name). So on the forms I had to lie, something that often made me inordinately uncomfortable. I had to say that, like my sister, I had a child. I worried that the doctor would notice it was not true, that my belly and breasts were too flat. It was yet another characteristic of my autism that I was all bent out of shape over this. But there was no need to concern myself, instead a deficiency in white blood cells showed up and I was told I had leukemia.

There was no time to study this further because I went back to France. My twelve-year-old niece was sometimes difficult. She once locked me out of the house and I was left in tears walking around in the bitter cold until I found a church where to warm myself up for a few hours.

The French doctors decided it must be mononucleosis and they left me alone, thankfully. Nothing could be found to treat me. Mononucleosis did not explain the fainting but I was certainly having hypoglycemic reactions—dizziness, fatigue and fainting. Since nothing worse appeared to happen my symptoms were no longer medically attended. For many years all I knew was that I had a tendency to become weak and pass out.

My mother then arranged for me to live for a while with two social-worker friends of hers in Paris who were sisters. They let me stay at their place and found me a job in the big Parisian store called *Le Printemps*. I was a cashier in the department store. Counting the money in the register at the end of the day was a task I did well but in the social area it was another matter. I was not good with the public, my sales were terrible, and I did not become friends with any of my coworkers. Each day I dreaded the time when in the locker room I had to change and put on the work uniform (a long blouse) as each time the static electricity from the metal gave me a painful jolt. This, and the tension with others, soon scared me and I promptly quit.

The next day I devised another way to end it all and kill myself. I was fed up with my previous failed attempts, so I gave myself an ultimatum: there would be no more "half and half" and if I did not succeed this time I would find a way to ameliorate my life. The plan was to jump out the window of the sisters' apartment as it was located on a high floor. As I was ready to jump from the window a man appeared to watch me from across the building, and that was enough to deter me.

I am ashamed to think of how thoughtlessly I was going to reward the sisters for their help. The thought of how I was about to hurt the people around me at those times did not cross my mind. It took many years for me to become aware of others' feelings, but I did eventually and that process was thorough, if imperfect at times. It seems to me that autistic children ought to be given more time before they are judged as irremediably irresponsible. Also I do not think that the "normal" child is necessarily also so quick at thinking of how her actions will affect others. The way I see it, one of the major differences is that she is not labeled and thus no one makes a fuss over it, thereby giving a chance for the child to grow up in an environment which offers numerous opportunities.

Many years later I realized that I had been very fortunate to visit with two caring households; they helped give me the strength to get back on track. Back to the reality of my life, as I had promised myself, I now had to do something constructive about my life. The only way to start over was to bite the bullet and come back to my parents while I found the means to learn a trade and sustain myself. I had to really clench my teeth to do this and I crossed off every day on the calendar until I was able to leave my parents' home a few months later. I was unable to ask for help. I did not even know that I was allowed to ask, but my stubbornness was useful and I decided to forget all that fancy studying that may not lead anywhere and instead study something short and practical, something that would almost guarantee a job: secretarial skills. I figured a way to go back to a school for a two-year program in the nearest university town of Nantes.

The next two years I attended school at The College Vial in the city of Nantes. Nantes is about sixty kilometers away from les Sables d'Olonne. At the College Vial I learned secretarial skills in a program called BTS, *Brevet Technicien Supérieur*. The living arrangements in one of Nantes' public students dormitories were cheap enough for my parents not to balk at paying the required fee, and they probably were happy to see my determination.

These two years turned out to be the best ones when I lived in France as it was really the first time I lived alone (in the dormitory I had my own tiny bedroom) and I had the opportunity to further discover myself.

Rather than taking the crowded bus back and forth between school and dormitory, I biked for forty minutes twice a day on the bike a classmate of mine loaned to me. The long commute was hard on me at times, but it suited me and I successfully completed the program. My classmates were all girls several years younger than me and none of them lived in the public student dorms on the outskirts of Nantes; almost all of them went back to their parents' home every day after school. The only three girls who were my age often went out together but despite my willingness to go with them they never asked me to go along, which very much troubled me. The familiar, incomprehensible and seemingly unending rejection feelings surfaced again.

Mealtimes were supposed to be taken at the university cafeteria but I did not like to eat there. The few times I went, I had to walk doubled over because of the smell and the pain in my abdomen. Since I did not know about gastrointestinal pains and had never mentioned them to anyone— for what? Nobody understood it—I believed that my solar plexus was the problem. Instead of going to the cafeteria, I ate the same foods over and over in my small bedroom thanks to the burner I hid in my closet. In order to keep food refrigerated I hung a plastic bag outside the window at night. Many other students did the same and when looking out the window at night, one could see plastic bags outside of many windows of the dorms.

In the co-ed dorm I had to interact with many foreigners who were about my age. The two Arabs who lived directly across from one another on the same floor as me did not talk to one another and I was shocked to find out that they did not mingle with one another because back at home their clans were at war. Toward the end of my stay in the dormitory and after I had had several encounters with other Arabic students, I must have done something to offend them because suddenly the entire group, including my neighbors, decided to give me the cold shoulder.

Victor was a German student whom I later visited in Gottingen. He was studying in Nantes while writing a book on Jules Verne, which was published in 1986. Brendon and Chloe were Canadians. Brendon lighted his farts with his cigarette lighter, and Chloe and he were gay. I once spent a night with Chloe as I was ready to experience anything, hoping I might figure out that way what ailed me. The night left me quite unmoved and I slept.

On weekends most French students who resided at the dorm went back to their parents but I chose to stay at the dorm. During a weekend where I had stayed at the dormitory, three African students in the kitchen at the end of the hall were cooking fat black caterpillars. They offered some of this delicacy and since I did not want to offend them I took the tiniest bite and choked on it. I helped another friend put on makeup in the evening so he was able to roam around in the park all night long and chase men, and, afterward, seriously lacked sleep. He drew the cover page of my research report on feminism for the *dactylographie* or typing class. Thirty years later I would find out that, completely unbeknown to me, he was not fully gay and he had had a serious crush on me.

Jay, an American student doing a study-abroad program, became my boyfriend. With him I was finally able to go to a few student parties and get drunk out of my mind. Once I was so sick and for so long it discouraged me from alcohol binges forever. I had stopped taking the pill and I quickly became pregnant. My first abortion was performed in Nantes, France and at that time those were done without anesthesia. Jay came with me and I hardly remember the procedure, it paled in comparison with the other trauma in my life. When Jay went back to the United States, I had not yet completed my diploma and I wanted to finish what I had set to do with such difficulty. For a year we kept up a telephone relationship. Jay did not know if he was gay or heterosexual and I felt that gay people were more sensitive so that did not worry me so much.

When I graduated, the diploma I received was the first in a long series of diplomas that I would not really use professionally. However some of the skills I learned would often be practical and useful in my personal life (for example, at that time I learned typing). During these two years I saved the money my parents thought would be used to buy train tickets. Instead I hitchhiked the sixty kilometers it took to go visit them during school breaks. This allowed me to afford a one way plane ticket to Chicago, United States, where Jay lived.

When my parents found out I'd be leaving France for a country many miles away across the Atlantic, they did not put up any fuss. On the contrary I got the feeling they were relieved. My mother later told me that I had willfully and unreasonably severed all my ties to them, which seemed to justify the fact that she no longer felt responsible for me in any way once I was in United States. The romance with Jay provided a bridge between two countries. Though I did not process it consciously I knew I ought to find a different environment and I did not feel able to breathe properly in the French culture of that time.

PART II

CHICAGO

A YOUNG ADULT: 1987-1999

General Adaptation Syndrome Stage 2: Resistance

If the threat continues, the body adapts to the strains or demands of the stressor. However, the body cannot keep doing this indefinitely. Over time, the organism weakens and its resources are gradually depleted.

CHAPTER 10: FIRST IMPRESSIONS, FIRST MARRIAGE

Bridal shower, 1987

I immigrated to Chicago, United States of America, at the beginning of July 1987, two weeks after turning twenty-three years old. Jay picked me up at the airport. He did not have a car so we took the elevated train to his place. Between the racket of the train engine and the breaks that hissed each time the train came in a new station, it was too loud for conversation. I was overwhelmed with a mix of exhaustion and a feeling of unreality at the new sights and sounds. People spoke a language I did not understand and the sight of lined brick houses and alleys seen through dirty window panes was a complete novelty. Everyone was dressed and behaved differently, for example some of the women wore stockings—despite the heat and humidity, and gym shoes. For the next few months I felt like if I had landed on another planet.

In many ways the lifestyle change was a balm for my nerves. There was more flexibility in the United State, the many different cultures that had to coexist together promoted a kind of freedom I had never known previously. For one, food and eating customs were a major cultural novelty. I was often expected to use my fingers while eating and sometimes there was no silverware at all. The first time I went to a party at some of Jay's friends, I stared hungrily at the bowl of chips and salsa everyone around me helped themselves to, while I did not dare to. Many of the ethnic foods I had never tasted before were delicious. These foods were often radically different from the foods I was used to: Middle Eastern and Indian fare, Chicago's deep dish pizza, etc. Almost every Friday night Jay and I dined out, often at the same little Indian restaurant. We were allowed to bring our own bottle of wine and take away our left over food, which were customs unheard of in France. Supermarkets stayed opened all night; a week after my arrival I was able to go at two a.m. to buy a pink stomach medicine—which did not do much to relieve my gastrointestinal pains.

In movie theaters when the public laughed at something on the screen, I often remained impassive, even if I understood what it was about. Everyone one around me thought that it was due to the different sense of humor between the French and Americans, but once I learned about my autistic nature it came as no surprise to me to realize that this may have something to do with my different sense of humor.

For someone as sensory-challenged as me it was a real relief to be able to say hello and goodbye with a simple nod instead of the many greeting kisses I had experienced in France. Also, it was not considered rude to most often wear dark sun glasses and/or a hat. Hidden behind my sunglasses I relished the ability to stare incognito at the people whose behaviors so amazed me.

It took me a long time to get a grasp on the concept of health insurance in United State. A year after my arrival in United States, my knee was injured when a car knocked me over while I was walking across a street and the car sped away without stopping. I took it for granted that I received medical care, not understanding that I was in fact lucky to have health coverage thanks to my husband's plan.

The first six months after my arrival in the United States, Jay and I lived together. We hardly knew one another but we were young and blissfully unaware, we loved one another and getting married was logical. Furthermore my immigration status as an unmarried foreigner did not allow me to legally work and we needed my earnings. A few weeks before my wedding to Jay, his parents organized a bridal shower for me.

The concept of a bridal shower was completely new to me and did not exist in France. Never before had I received so many beautifully wrapped gifts. My amazement was utterly complete when I opened the gifts: half a dozen of them contained a negligee! What was I to do with all these negligees? The only time I put them on was for my own personal show when, alone in my bedroom the next day, I decided that I had no use for such uncomfortable and silly frills. I had been taught that a gift should never be gotten rid of and I was unaware of the U.S. relatively-relaxed store return policy but, anyhow, even once I knew of it I never dared to return anything. One negligee at a time I was forced to downsize my possessions due to my many moves and I gave them away to various friends.

My first part-time job was as a part-time waitress in a liberal little coffee shop near where we lived in Chicago's North side. Soon it became apparent that I was not very successful at it and that I was often clumsy. Once I bumped a customer while carrying a tray and the funny bone in my elbow hurt (What's so funny about pain?). I said "*aïe*," which is the French sound for "ouch," but the customer thought I said "hi." Even more inappropriate were my daily long talks with a Vietnam War veteran whose stories kept me spellbound. I had never heard of the Vietnam War before and he had lost his foot on the day I was born! I was a terrible salesperson and rather than increase the customer's bill, I always tried to lessen it. The owners of the café gave me less and less work hours and eventually I stopped working there. I wondered what I had done wrong but it took me many years to understand that the above situations may have been some of the reasons.

Once Jay and I started to live together and got to know one another a little better, our differences clearly showed and we started to argue a lot. The first episode I remember that brought up a serious divide in our relationship happened only a few weeks after my arrival in United States. Jay and I were biking in the forest of a Chicago suburb on the way to his parents. Jay, who knew the place well, sped away and disappeared from my sight. Alone in a deep and unknown forest I became extremely frightened and overwhelmed. Several times I called for Jay at the top of my lungs but there was no answer and I kept going haphazardly, blinded by my tears while fueled by fear and anger. When, after what seemed to me like ages, Jay finally returned to look for me, I blew a fuse and became enraged. I think this was the first time Jay witnessed how undone I could become, and the sudden boiling over that showed my true nature must have been frightening to him.

Another time, after we had an argument and I became frightfully enraged (unfortunately I was good at this!), Jay tied my hands together and left there. When he cut me loose less than an hour later, I was so upset that I once again lost it and hurt myself. I purposely took a knife and cut the skin on my right index finger, about half a centimeter. I have always been in the habit of feeling so lost and worthless at times that I believed I ought to die. The scar of this self-inflicted injury is still faintly visible almost thirty years later. When I regained lucidity, I decided that I could not stay in a marriage where such things happened to me. I went to a legal agency and used up all my recently earned money to ask for a divorce. Jay agreed and only six months after our marriage we were legally divorced.

My Green Card immigrant status was at risk and I had to prove to the Chicago Immigration and Naturalization Services that I had married without an ulterior motive to establish myself in the United States. In order to do this much tedious paperwork had to be done: bank account statements, affidavits from various friends, etc. It all seemed silly to me, as if one could prove that kind of thing, but I nevertheless put the required file together following in detail the written guidelines.

The ability to do detailed work is one of the great traits of my autism. The only part of the process that was real to me was the oath which took place once I had completed the paperwork. I had to swear I had emigrated in good faith, which did not worry me since it was true. I believe it is a characteristic of many an autistic individual that one remains as truthful as possible to the bottom line, even when circumstances require more finesse. In any event this was a straightforward issue: I had come to the United States in good faith so I could take the oath in complete sincerity.

CHAPTER 11: HEALTHIER AND CONSTANTLY MOVING

Hoping to keep away the many challenges for which I had no name and no explanation, I became healthier. Diet was the first thing that I cleaned up. My first husband was vegetarian and it was easy for me to follow suit since already I disliked meat. Today, I am still vegetarian.

Cycling was another habit good for my health. I already had often used my bike in France and when I noticed that many of the people I knew biked in Chicago I got over my intimidation of the big American city. Chicago has some beautiful flat public bicycle paths.

I tried to play tennis again. Many of my tennis friends thought I ought to competitively play since I was so skilled. They did not understand my reluctance to do so and I did not know how to explain that the stress of competition anguished me so much it impaired my game. A few times I complied with my friends and entered a tournament in Chicago. Each time the experience left me with a bitter taste. One tournament was in an indoor facility and the familiar "indoor noise" very much affected me. During most of the match my stomach was knotted and a few times I imperceptibly tripped. Even though I was stronger than my opponent I lost the match. However I yearned for intense physical activity and wondered what could replace tennis. It would have to be something non-competitive and practiced in a quiet environment. I had been in United States for a year when a colleague introduced me to yoga.

Dan, my yoga teacher for the next eleven years, taught in a way that suited me. He taught his classes in silence, without the musical tunes which can seriously grate on my nerves. His own studio had large windows allowed enough daylight to come in during the day, and in the evenings he covered the fluorescent lights with cotton drapes that were hung a few inches away from the bulbs. On top of the regular sweaty sessions I attended at this studio a few times a week, for the next three years I also attended several intense yoga workshops under the guidance of renowned yoga teachers. A few times I experienced the familiar physical sensation of dizziness and once I came close to fainting, but I learned to stop and put my head down when I felt like this; only one or two times did I need to I step outside the class to sit down for a few minutes. The overall well-being I experienced easily overrode the negative effects. Yoga gave me a powerful means to release my inner tension, and to this day I have kept up a daily yoga routine at home first thing in the morning.

At a yoga workshop in a Catholic seminary for men I was once extremely mortified. It was a pleasantly warm spring day and during a break for the intense schedule my friend and I decided to rollerblade around the seemingly empty campus. I was going to visit my hometown in France shortly after and I wanted to be tan in order to fit in on the beach, so on that day I only wore my French bathing suit. I did not realize that there was silent meditation going on nearby and that we were seen. Soon one of the seminary men came to ask me to cover myself up, which so ashamed me that I immediately stopped roller-blading and never forgot the incident.

With relative ease I picked up my adopted country's new ways and learned to play the social game, pretending to blend in. Though for several months I felt like if I was on another planet, I quickly picked up on some of the accents of my new home's language. Many of the people who heard me speak and heard my accent, could not pin where it was from exactly. When they asked about it, for many years I thought it was funny to let them guess: they often thought I was from a European country like Germany or Poland, and it was usually not until I took on purpose an exaggerated thick French accent that they figured it out. I attribute this ability to pick up the nuances of an accent to my autism; it has often been documented how some autistic children can easily learn a foreign language and/or mimic an accent.

I still believed that everyone had the same challenges as me, and lived and slept constantly nervous in a vivid and intense inner world. As far as I knew, I *was* the person I was pretending to be. I thought that if only I clenched my teeth hard enough and shut out my many discomforts, I was going to will away my challenges.

The following two years I moved around a lot. Because I now worked full-time I was able to earn some money and support myself. In the United States, it seemed to me that my differences were more acceptable, and that I could at least hope to find my way around somehow. In hindsight I can see that I did, but I always "limped." Nobody in my French family offered to support or help in any way; I really did not keep them well informed and never asked anything, not because I did not feel the need to but rather because I was unable to. My sister had long settled in Canada and she offered me to come and live with her and her daughter. I asked for a transfer at work but this was refused.

For a few weeks I found shelter with a married French woman with two young children. I helped out with the children and it seemed to me that all went fine. I was stunned when she suddenly asked me to leave and refused to speak with me ever again. I had to promptly find another place. Joan, who was about my age, needed a roommate because she had just broken up with her boyfriend. I had met her while we were both waitresses. For the next six months or so, I slept in the living room of her one bedroom apartment. At her place I experienced for the first time in my life—but not the last—the bitter taste of being alone when it seems that everyone else celebrates and I was envious of Joan, who had parents to help her. Her mother gathered the family during the holidays (I was invited but Jennifer did not want me to go) and when Joan's father helped her pay the rent, she asked me to leave.

After my failed shared-living attempts, I moved into the Chicago down-town Y.M.C.A, where I had my own bedroom and I was independent. I no longer had to contend with the failed expectations of the other people I lived with. As a bonus, it was an inexpensive place closer to my job. While I lived there I met a French-speaking Arab taxi driver who also lived at the YMCA. I was working full time and he talked me into lending him money. But several months later he still had not reimbursed me. Five hundred dollars was a lot for me as I really was not in a situation to be able to spare any money. The only strategy I was able to come up with was to intimidate him. This is often the only last resort defense I have when dire circumstances force me to it.

At the crack of dawn on a Sunday morning, two African-American work friends came with me to knock on his door at the YMCA. I hoped it would be such an unexpected surprise that it would get me some results. That morning, instead of being eaten by resentment and not knowing what to say about it, I worked up quite a rage. I did not knock, I pounded on his door. We woke him up and must have scared him out of his wits, which was the point: on the spot he gave me back the entire sum in cash. My friend Joan, who also had lent him five hundred dollars, never saw her money again. This YMCA was not very clean, one night I woke up suddenly because I had felt something: a huge cockroach was trailing on my thigh. And so I decided to move again.

For the next few months I lived with a co-worker I was in love with. Unfortunately my love was not returned as he was in love with an older Irish man. In hindsight thirty years later, I now realize that he only wanted to share his apartment with me because he needed help paying the rent. I was now earning enough money to be able to afford the rent for my own studio apartment and that is what I did.

Pretending to follow the invisible rules of the social game took a huge toll on me and after a while this always showed; one day my difficulties in adapting to change and handling stress flared up, and the unexpected behaviors that came with it became an unwelcome surprise to whoever lived around me.

CHAPTER 12: SHORT-LIVED, FULL-TIME JOBS AND SECOND MARRIAGE

I designed my own wedding invitation

During my first full-time job as an export clerk in a printing company, we were almost all immigrants in my office. In the factory across the street most workers were African-American and I was taken in by their warmth. Many seem to be willing to practically help me out and I felt a singular kinship, maybe due to the fact we felt, albeit in a diverse way, "different." Due to my inordinate ability to go through paperwork in detail—the dogged streak that is often an autistic characteristic, I soon became the person in the office who was known as the employee able to find the misplaced lost document, like the proverbial needle in a stack of hay. My different ways and behaviors were at first understood to be due to my being French and therefore their freshness was pleasing enough. For example, when I wrongly accentuated the word "purchasing" everyone had a good laugh. But before long people stopped being amused and became uncomfortable; less than eighteen months later I was asked to leave. However the company was in the process of closing down (it did so less than a year later) and though I was amongst the first to be let go, I did not feel too bad about being fired.

I wanted a change from the export business and for my second full-time blue-collar job I became a weight loss counselor at Jenny Craig, Inc. At first I was successful at it. Spending time one-on-one with the client during our counseling sessions allowed me to be less nervous, and I was often able to empathize and give ideas on how to try to overcome a problem. After all my own struggles had started to teach me to do this from a very young age—though I was still very far from having perfected it. The Jenny Craig, Inc. branch in Chicago decided to try me in a better-paid sales position. But when trying to sell the weight-loss program I was filled with the fear that I did not have the right to ask people to use up their hard-won money. I have always been very poor at sales and I do not have "the nerve" for it. When my failure to achieve the sales quota proved to be an enduring thing I was asked to either go back to counseling with a rather large pay cut, or leave. I chose to leave as I had become too uncomfortable to stick it out. Overall my stint at Jenny Craig, Inc. lasted less than a year.

I soon found a third full-time job in the export department of a drilling bits and equipment factory. It was to be my third (and last) blue-collar job in United States. My boss was open-minded and left me to my own devices. My desk was away from the others and as always at first I was not so irritated by the social aspects of the job. However after a year and a half my mood changed, I was pregnant and several incidents increased my uneasiness.

First, a worker from the factory came in the office and was yelled at by the big boss for walking over the office rug in his boots. To me, the rug was already quite ragged and stained and the boss, who was usually absent anyway, had an uncalled for patronizing attitude. A few days after this, a new salesman in the export department was hired. He and I immediately clashed and I chose to quit on the day he asked me to make his coffee. I did not know how to make it, and did not want to learn to make because I felt it was overly expected of women (by then I was also ten months pregnant).

My experience with jobs was that I became so uncomfortable that, after only a few months, if I was not asked to leave beforehand, I often terminated them myself. A terrible uneasiness eventually took over, despite that I always did my best to do exactly what was required. For example I was always on time and paid attention to my clothes. I did not yet understand that all public and social contact made me uneasy, that I needed an inordinate amount of quiet. I later realized that my different ways were often perceived as a threat.

In any event, I started to learn that in the United States some job ethics are different than in France. For example I could be hired and fired almost the same day without further ado. However there is a more appealing facet to this: for people like me, who may be quickly overwhelmed with a job situation, to be able to terminate and switch jobs rather quickly can be a kind of ticket to a limping survival.

Next, I rented out a studio and this lonely living arrangement greatly improved my moods. I only had a mattress to sleep on and very little furniture but I finally lived alone and did not have to be social in my own space. As such I finally was able to relax some, to recharge my batteries and regain more energy.

While I was living there I met Simon, who would become my second husband and the father of my only child. We met while we were sitting next to one another as spectators at a tennis championship event. Our first date was to play tennis together and I was then reminded of my mother telling me many years ago in France that "tennis opens doors."

When the final interview with Immigration and Naturalization Services came I asked to meet with a person high in the INS hierarchy, as the saying "better speak to God than to his Saints" made perfect sense to me. I had already I had started to figure out that I had better chances of being understood if I spoke to the most experienced person on board, for example the boss. She might be less quick to assume the wrong thing. Also, Simon accompanied me and told the INS boss how much he hoped that I be allowed to stay. Between these and my detailed paperwork, I was able to keep the Green Card status that allowed me to be a legal immigrant.

Simon was living in a basement apartment while his sister lived in the upstairs apartment of the same condominium. After about six months of courting I moved in with him, not realizing that the condo belonged to his mother and she was our landlord. There were five buildings in our condominium association and Simon was born in another one of them. He and his family had strong ties in the association and I was the newcomer on the block.

Simon and I decided to remodel our basement apartment, which I did not realize until years later was a way for Simon to trade for rent with his mother and to have cheap help while doing it. The fumes of the chemicals we used made me sick and for the first time in my life (but not the last!) I had to wear a face mask. After the remodeling, the place looked much better and though I was never thanked for my work I felt responsible and worked hard at keeping it clean and clear of all clutter.

I became pregnant almost immediately after meeting Simon. He was older, had previously been married and divorced and had a ten year old daughter who lived with her mother in Ohio. Scared by my previous marital experience, I felt it was too early in our relationship to know if this was going to be a stable one and I was not so sure about my ability to be a good mother. And so for the second time in my life I chose to abort, a decision I have never regretted.

During yet another visit to my family of origin (at that time I went back to France every two or three years), Simon and I went camping on l'Ile d'Yeu, a beautiful island a few hours away from les Sables d'Olonne, my hometown. One morning while there, I woke up unable to move my neck and in severe pain. I could only see a doctor several days later, once we were back in my hometown. By then much of the acuity of the pain had disappeared and the doctor only thought it was due to the cold floor. He prescribed a neck brace and after several weeks the pain went away. But in hindsight I wonder if this may have been a precursor of the paralyzing and unbearable neck and back cramp I would experience in my forties.

I always strived to appear to be like everyone else and I thought I ought to be married. Simon agreed to do so and our wedding took place in a church, both liberal enough to accommodate my second husband's tastes while traditional enough for his mother. A small party of friends attended the reception in the building adjoining the church. I felt uncomfortable and stuffed up in the white and scratchy dress; the high heels and make-up did not feel like me. But I was not about to upset my new mother-in-law, whom I already feared was not too happy with me. I designed the wedding invitations' image. I soon was pregnant again, and this time I kept the child I was bearing. I now felt ready to be a mother, since I was married, felt stable, and was at an age where it was expected to have children.

Just before the birth, Simon and I bought the condominium on the first floor directly above us. It had three bedrooms and was much bigger than the small one-bedroom basement apartment we lived in. My new husband had known the former owners his entire life and was like an adopted child in their childless lives. When the man died and his widow was too ill to take care of it, the apartment was sold to Simon for a good price. I once visited the widow in her nursing home and her pitiful tears at my visit (I don't think she had many visitors) made me also tear up. I then saw how important it is to visit friends and older people who find themselves alone and away from home.

When I was about ten months pregnant I stopped working and stayed home until my son's birth, at which time I immediately started to attend the nearby university (in fact I had my son only a few days before my first class). My husband, his father and his mother were all teachers so my husband suggested I follow suit and become a teacher. Going back to school suited me: like so many autistic individuals I enjoyed its structure and was relieved at not being as pressed to perform as in a work situation.

In order to be accepted into the university, I first had to pass an examination that all students who went back to school after a hiatus, or who came from a foreign country, had to take: the English Competency Examination. For the first time in my life I was confronted with the "fill in the circle" test forms. I did not know what to do and I panicked when I saw everyone around me had started. When I finally thought to read the written explanations it suddenly made sense—which may be another useful learning tip for an autistic individual: always read the fine print. The multiple-choice system was far easier than what I had known. For the essay part I was surprised to observe that many of my fellow students did not use scratch paper. How were they able to organize their thoughts in a clear manner without being able to see their thoughts on paper? I could not do this, so I wrote my essay according to the system I had been taught, and I passed the test! I was proud of this achievement. I had heard of born-and-raised American individuals who had not passed the examination, while I had immigrated only five years ago.

CHAPTER 13: BIRTH OF A SON AND STRESSED RELATIONSHIP

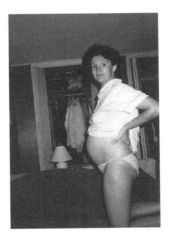

I am pregnant, 1991

It was fortunate that my husband wanted the birth to take place in our home, as I was scared of hospitals which, in hindsight, I understand to be due to the increased sensory overload in hospitals (more noises, more lights, more smells, more movement, etc.). Though the beginning the birthing process was uneventful, by the time the baby's head was showing I had lost all my already depleted strength and was unable to push the baby past my fused lumbar. The midwife performed an episiotomy without anesthetics, but when this did not work she started to get ready to bring me to the nearby hospital in order to perform a Cesarean surgery. At that moment my husband had the brilliant idea to feed me fresh orange slices in order to give me energy. I then had enough strength for a final push. I fainted but the baby came out unharmed. The oxygen delivered by mask revived me and from then on I would have great admiration for the power of oxygen.

We named our son Matthieu. It was marvelous to have such a complete connection with my son, such a wonder, while at the same time it increased my sensory challenges ten times. The baby's cries, the smells of dirty cloth diapers and the lack of sleep stressed my frayed nerves. I got up every few hours during the night to nurse and change the quickly soaked cloth diapers and my already difficult sleep became even lighter. I started to wear earplugs during the night. Nonetheless, at the least noise in the baby's room (his crib was on the other side of the contingent wall) I was up –even if it turned out to be useless- and did not go back to sleep for a long time.

I was only able to breastfeed the baby for about three weeks. I was so sensitive that my nipples often bled despite the stinky Lanolin cream and the nursing coach who made sure that the baby and I did it "the right way." One day when nursing, I saw my toes all curled up like if I was being tortured. It dawned on me that no matter how other people, including my husband, sang the praises of breastfeeding, it could not be good for the baby to have his mother in such pain, and I then dared to stop breastfeeding.

The many visits to the doctor were yet another challenge. I had to first call and make an appointment, at which time I was often put on hold for a long time. Then had to explain myself quickly to a complete stranger. Once this was done, I had to arrange for transportation for the baby and me, since we only had one car and my husband usually used it to go to work. Once in the crowded and noisy waiting room I had to keep my active son quiet while I fought off the overwhelming sensory feedback.

I was so tired that I sorely felt the need for help, any kind of help. I envied my husband for being so often away at work. My mother in law often came from South California to visit us. I am grateful for the one-week long break I had thanks to her the year after my son's birth. Lydia my sweet twelve year old step daughter, also helped as much as she could when she visited us during school vacations. Both my mother and my aunt Sylvie came from France, at different times, and for short visits. However no one stayed long enough to allow me the regular respite I yearned for and this further increased my resentment toward the one family member who lived nearby and did not work, my husband's sister.

At the time I thought her refusal to help with the baby was only because she resented me. When she had to be with me during holiday celebrations she often expressed anger at me for upsetting her brother. It was only when I left Chicago and my son was older and more independent that she started to spend time with him. In retrospect I realized that she was herself ill and I now think she must have had her own reasons for her behavior.

Before my son was old enough to go to a daycare program I either scheduled my university classes while his father was at home in the evenings, or the neighbor's teenage daughter babysat for us. I was relieved when Matthieu was eighteen months old and he was comfortable attending my university's daycare program.

Without a car I often had to bring Matthieu to the daycare on my bike, which could be grueling. I still remember the cold days when, already exhausted, I dressed him warmly in his snow suit, carried the bike up the flight of stairs from the basement and installed the baby seat at the rear of the bike, all the while checking that my little one did not run into the nearby street. At last I fastened him securely in his seat, put on both our helmets (I had never worn one before but I felt I was the role model), and off we went. I was careful to keep the bike wheels inside the cars' snow tracks and walked the bike in slippery places.

A few months after Matthieu's birth, I registered him as a French citizen. Though in order to do this I had to face the challenge of going a few times by public transportation to the downtown Chicago French Consulate over an hour away. I thought Matthieu might really appreciate the opportunity of having dual citizenship once he was older—and he did.

Despite the economic, mental and physical toll on me to visit the place where I always had to pretend to be conventional, I also thought it was important that Matthieu's French grandmother and grandfather meet him. Thus when Matthieu was only six months old we flew to visit them in France. Matthieu's father only came two weeks later, but my twelve years old step daughter Lydia was with me and she was good with the baby. As soon as I saw the city of Paris through the plane windows, painful anxiety butterflies formed in my stomach.

My mother, who I forever thought to be unhappy with me, did not like the way I cared for Matthieu and thought I spoiled him. She resented that I kept him in the backpack while I attended my daily chores and that I ate many meals standing up, rocking from side to side. Once she manipulated me into leaving the baby crying for hours in his crib where he was supposed to take a nap and later I very much regretted that I gave in. My mother also resented the fact that I am vegetarian, which required her to alter her cooking. The stress of what I understood to be constant disapproval weighed heavily on me. Much later I realized it might only be a "grudging habit," and that I had also taken on that habit.

This visit was the first and last time Matthieu met my father as he died less than a year later. Frustrated that I could not attend his funeral, I looked instead into the story of his life as a convict and learned many details that neither my mother nor the book _Papillon_ had taught me when I was younger.

First I figured how to contact a journalist familiar with my father's trial and he sent me a book on the penitentiary in French Guyana, along with two yellowish newspaper articles about my father. I learned that the entire penitentiary is mostly on the city of Cayenne and that Devil Island is a nearby island where the convicts whose cases were political and had been heard of by the French public (including my father's) were sent. French Guyana's convicts often died, either from the heat, Malaria, the sharks or other accidents that were often not properly treated. Doubtless because he was one of the few able to read and write, my father became the secretary for the "_commandant supérieur_" (the superior commander), which was a "*placarde*," a favored position. The movie *Papillon* (based on the book), with famous actors Steve McQueen and Dustin Hoffman, is about the French Guyana penitentiary.

Until my son was old enough to fend for himself a little, like most every mother—whether neuro-typical or autistic—nothing else but taking care of him existed for me. In the case of autistic me, it also meant that I had no space left for anything else and I was on automatic pilot more than usual, and unable to pay attention to any of my many discomforts. Consequently, I often exhibited much distress and sadness, but it was misunderstood by all, including my husband. Much strife occurred in our relationship, but for the sake of privacy I will only give a few tame examples of this. Because I was so tired I had started to take naps in the afternoons, but it took me forever to fall asleep and if I managed it, I woke up in a dark mood. He rather sarcastically took to calling them "beauty naps."

One day Matthieu was crying hard and I sensed it was because something hurt him, so I wanted to take him to the doctor to be checked. Typically, I was unable to explain this clearly and instead all I managed to do was to be upset as my son's dark mood invaded me. Naturally it made things worse, and at first Simon flatly refused take us to the doctor. He thought that Matthieu's pain would go away by itself and that I made too much fuss about it. In the end he gave in, declaring angrily that he was only doing it for my sake, because I was such a pain. It turned out Matthieu, always prone to earaches, had both ears infected and strong antibiotics were prescribed.

When Simon listened to the football games on the television, the noise of the yelling and the excited commentator's voice gave me a headache. Thus Simon had to wear a headset, an accommodation he resented, especially since I did not have a medical explanation for it yet. Eventually, he seemed to find escape in his work. He took over two other little part time jobs and sometimes other projects, and as such was hardly ever home. I felt I had to do all of the baby's care by myself.

I was so depressed that I was once again visited by thoughts of suicide. One day I asked Simon if he knew of a good spot to kill myself on train tracks: the El Train was not too far from where we lived and Simon then took me to a suitable spot. I was about to lie down on the tracks when the thought of my little son—left alone with the huge emotional trauma of his mother's suicide—brought me back to a saner view of reality. I remembered a French girlfriend's grief when she told me how much her father's suicide affected her still, though she was in her forties. For a moment there I was back at my parent's, and just like I had let my dad think whatever he wanted that day long ago, I let my husband believe whatever he wanted to. I let him believe that he had been correct in thinking this was only manipulation of my part, that I really did not mean to kill myself. At the time I thought (and it enraged me) that by leading me thus to the train tracks he only wanted to prove me wrong. But I am no longer so sure nowadays since almost twenty years later he told me that he also thought of suicide that day.

A few months after my son's birth, I once again found myself pregnant. However it was not at all intended, on the contrary. Since I really did not have the strength to care for another child, I had yet another abortion, my third and last one. Many years later, I am still really glad I had these three abortions; they made my (and Matthieu's!) life possible. Given that taking care of just one child took such a toll on me, I believe that I would not have been able to handle more. I don't think it would be fair to the young women like me to take the abortion option away.

The doctor I was seeing at the time prescribed some mild anti-depressants but they did seem to have much of an effect. She then referred my husband and me to meet with a marital counselor. So for a few months, I arranged for a babysitter and dragged my reluctant husband to see Dr. Z. every other week. At least two times Simon forgot we had an appointment and I waited for him in the freezing cold. The marriage counselor did not either understand the larger picture of my autism and he believed I was depressed mainly because of my difficult relationship. Nevertheless, the session helped me realize that my marriage negatively and deeply affected me.

For many months I toyed with the thought of divorce but I did not dare bring it up. However, once I could independently earn enough money to support my son, I was emboldened. When my husband uttered the divorce word, I jumped at the opportunity. I had secured a teaching job for the summer and I took the plunge. The day I moved away, I was so intent on doing it all alone that I damaged the rented truck's right mirror.

I never once regretted the decision to move out, though being completely on my own and having a son to support was extremely difficult many times. I knew that I too must have somehow been responsible for the failure of my second marriage. But all I could understand at that time is that my chemistry make-up was caustic to others and that people who entered in contact with this chemical got burnt, and so did I.

CHAPTER 14: FINISHING MY STUDIES AND BECOMING A SINGLE MOTHER

While juggling childcare and my relationship, I kept at my study goals. Mathematics was my most difficult subject. In order to remediate this, I carried a pen and a Kumon algebra math workbook (which presents algebra skills in an intuitive sequence) everywhere. Each time I had time to spare, standing in line, in a waiting room, in another class or while my son was napping, I completed more of the workbooks' problems and the level of difficulty increased. Motivated and left alone to my own device, with the constant repetition and slow increase in difficulty I was eventually able to complete the university mathematic requirements for a B.A.

When the time came for me to choose a specific subject to teach at a high school level, I chose French because I was confident that I knew this topic. But I was not allowed to take French higher level classes at my university because I did not have the necessary United States credentials. A long process started. First I had to ask Educational Credential Evaluators, Inc. to assess that I had the equivalent of an Associate of Applied Science degree in French.

After this I applied for a non-traditional degree in French at the Board of Governors program of my university. Ironically, the program required that I only claimed skills I had acquired after I was eighteen years old. In a portfolio aiming to show my French skills, I was thus forced to claim that I had learned most of the French I knew after when I went to a French university. The examining French teacher, who could tell that I had been raised in France since birth as I was so fluent, thought that this was hilarious. But he well understood that I had to do this and he could attest that I indeed knew my subject, which is what really mattered in the end. At last I was allowed to take the few French classes of higher level that allowed me to complete my B.A. in December 1993.

I started to teach part-time as soon as I had earned enough school credits to allow for it. At first I was only allowed to teach in private schools, and once a week for three months I taught an adult class at the Chicago French consulate. Two of my students became good friends and later helped me several times. One of them told me he learned a lot during the French classes he took with me as his teacher. But the consulate people must have felt differently for, though I applied, they did not rehire me for the next trimester.

This failure bothered me but I enjoyed working with adult students, so I started to teach French adults classes with the Berlitz language program. A few months later, and since they knew of my imminent teaching certificate, Berlitz asked me to teach part time in an elementary school in a suburb of Chicago. The job offered more hours and more money so I took it, but I soon found out that motivating young students and enforcing discipline was more challenging. Also it was a long two-hour drive to the school, and the day when I lost control of my car in a snow storm I realized the job was not worth it.

In May 1995, I completed an Illinois State approved Teaching Certificate in French. In order to teach in the state of Illinois in any subject other than English as a Second Language, United States Citizenship was required. When taking another country's citizenship, an individual can sometimes be torn between his family and country or origin and the country of emigration. However I did not have to abandon my native French citizenship in order to take the U.S. citizenship, France allows dual citizenship. Once I had taken the U.S. citizenship, I was legally able to substitute-teach older children in Illinois public high schools.

After I had separated, several friends advised me to move back to France. But I remembered far too well the constant stress to have to conform, and how uneasy illness had followed. Furthermore, the thought of how Simon would feel if Matthieu was raised in a far-away land that was expensive to visit, and where everyone spoke a foreign language and had different values and customs, was too horrifying for me to consider putting him through. In this way I was loyal, even if I experienced "irremediable differences" with him. Thus for the next three years, Simon and I shared the custody of our son. Matthieu stayed one week with me and the next one he went to be with his father and his paternal grandmother, who had moved in with her grown son the day after I had moved out.

The year after our separation, I rented an apartment that was close to Simon's place so as to make the transition as easy as possible for Matthieu. He could keep going to same school as before, a private French school where we had obtained for him a scholarship the year before. Matthieu's American grandmother helped take care of him while he was at his father's, and this helped reassure the mother in me that he was "safe." At the French school I met both French families and teachers, and during the next three summers I was the French summer-camp tennis teacher and could bring Matthieu with me.

I did not have time to go to yoga classes so, at home and by myself, I started to do fifteen minutes of yoga first thing every morning. On days when I did not work and had more time, I practiced for longer periods. This became my daily morning routine that I kept up for many years afterwards. I believe that yoga has been my first "serious" health benefit.

At that time in my life, I stayed away from French-North-American immigrant social groups because I felt so burnt about France and French people. But after the separation I realized that French people might be a family of sorts for my son and me. So I went with five-year-old Matthieu to a gathering of French people during the French custom *Galette des Rois*, or Twelfth Night Cake. There I met Patricia, an older wealthy French woman who would, for the next twenty years, become a second mother to me.

After the separation with my husband I kept the older of our two cars, but I completely wrecked it only a few months later. Luckily my son was not in the car when it happened and neither the other driver (who had made a too-fast turn right in front of me) nor I was injured. I remember from the accident that I was tired and in a hurry that day, and that the other driver complained of whiplash long after the accident itself, which made my insurance costs go up.

The famously-difficult intersection where the accident happened was next to a car dealer and I needed a car immediately in order to drive Matthieu here and there. Not only did I buy a used car there, I had a short-lived affair with the car dealer who seemed to like me. I thought that sleeping with him would ensure that the car I bought would be sound, but it turned out to be a lemon anyway. This man lived somewhere in the countryside of Chicago, and the one night we slept together at his place, I was unable to fall asleep due to his noisy snores. I abruptly left in the middle of the night, leaving a scant note on the kitchen table to say that I had left. When the car stopped working a few months later I went to another garage and I never saw the man again.

As had been my pattern before, I was hopelessly drawn into sexual relationships as soon as a man expressed interest in me, which I hoped to be love. I did not want to take a chance and become pregnant again, so soon after the divorce I asked my doctor to refer me for a tubal ligation. True to my prior promiscuity policy, during the next three years I had five brief sexual encounters: the handsome, young drug addict across from my apartment; the used car dealer; the ex-marine; the Hispanic illegal immigrant (who was really the nicest); and the African-American recently-divorced father of three children. I was fortunate never to be asked to do illegal business; I have heard that many autistics were not so lucky and were pulled into it sometimes without really understanding. I wonder if autistic women may be vulnerable to acting out sexually or being sexually abused while autistic men may be vulnerable to being the victims of illegal schemes. Whatever the case is, both autistic men and women may also be extremely intent on following rules, oftentimes displaying Obsessive Compulsive Disorder traits.

In order to try to figure out what was wrong with me and to see if I could get help with my extreme nervousness, I went to see several psycho-therapists. As always, making an appointment, waiting in crowded rooms and the timed visits was very stressful. The therapists were always kind women, but also seemed conditioned to give out advice without questioning the reality they knew or the assumptions they often made. Autism was still quite unknown and they didn't realize that my symptoms corresponded to autism.

My autism was made more difficult to diagnose by the fact that I did not convey very well what was going on (after all, I did not understand it myself), and the psychotherapists assumed I was mentally "normal" since I was raising my child and spoke a second language so well. They sometimes gave me some anti-depressants but I did not trust medication to address the root of a problem that was not understood. Each time the therapies were only superficial and did not appear to have much of an impact on me. In the end I did not have much time or money, and my unstable living arrangements made it difficult to sustain a long term therapy.

Without the support network of friends and family one has known for many years, caring for my child, finding jobs, moving in and out of apartments, and car problems consumed me.

CHAPTER 15: A CHALLENGING FIRST YEAR TEACHING

On the first day of the academic school year, I sat in the office of one of the better Chicago inner-city high schools; I had already spent the summer teaching French in that school and I was supposed to be working there for at least the duration of the year. While I waited I was on pins and needles, impatient to find out more about my job for the next school year. But a long time elapsed while I sat anxiously waiting to be told where to go without daring to ask. Would things have turned out differently if I had? Finally I was told that the former teacher had come back and that since she had priority over me I was "bumped out" (school jargon for, in short, no longer wanted). In shock, I immediately feared that, like so many times before, my performance during the summer did not endear me to the school, and being unable to figure out why was frustrating.

Unexpectedly I found myself without a job just after the divorce and with a five-years-old son to care for. Because I had felt safe enough to visit my family in France the month before, I had no money to pay the next month's rent and I will never forget the anguish I experienced then. Once I was in my car, safely surrounded by the noise of the other cars on the expressway, I screamed until my throat was too sore for it and then I sobbed for the entire time I was driving, about an hour.

After I had been bumped out of the promised job at the very last minute, I sat dejectedly in the office of the Chicago school board with a long line of other teachers, all waiting to see if we could find a job at the beginning of the school year. After three horrendous days of waiting, I was granted an interview with another high school in one of the most dangerous neighborhood in Chicago's south side. This school's principal was about to refuse the inexperienced and naive white young woman in front of him, and I was thus forced to betray my despair, that I had a young child to take care of and no back up money. Maybe spurred by empathy, he hired me.

This experience was a wake-up call. The stories my students told were often a reality check, reminding me that I was not the only one with problems. Until then I had lived in a white person's privileged middle-class environment and had almost no knowledge about African-American culture and history. I tried to listen to my students' stories despite the other teachers' warnings that they were so eager for attention that they exaggerated. Maybe it was so, but I did not think that the few students who may have exaggerated mattered so much when compared with the many who, in fact, were helped by relieving a little of their difficult circumstances.

While I listened to their stories I realized that money was almost always a problem and that my students often lived in stressful home situations with, for example, only one parent and many siblings or with a step parent or a grandmother. To tell all the stories I heard would be too long, but even with discounting some exaggerated and made-up stories, one thing was clear: every day brought its new tragedy for some student or another. I was often very sad on my students' behalf and my lack of protective filter allowed the stories to seep inside me deeply. It appeared to me that the students' acting out was a cry for help. The title of Bob Marley's song "Hallelujah" started to haunt me, with its lyrics about hearing the children crying.

A month after I had started teaching in this school one of my students, Charles, was killed. I decided to show my support and grief and go to his wake. I was surprised that only one teacher and one student from the school came with. At the school's door, the security man mumbled something that sounded like a warning, but I had no idea what he was talking about. When the three of us entered the wake building I noticed I was the only white person; I thought maybe it was yet early and they would arrive later. But that did not happen and when the bereaved student's grandmother got on the podium to give a speech and started to angrily talk about gangs and blame the white people, it dawned on me that the murder was a gang-related accident and lots of the audience was probably part of a gang. The tension started to build up and I started to become scared. May be sensing that this tension could become dangerous, the other teacher had us leave early. As we walked out between the rows of people whose anger about white people gave me goose bumps, images of my life and young son flashed by. I was grateful for my long black raincoat and my thick dark hair and I hid my white-skinned hands in my deep coat pockets. I am grateful to this teacher, whom I heard (through my friend Melanie) was later beaten up by some students and was in chronic pain afterwards.

A few months later my wallet was taken from the black briefcase I kept under my desk. I suspected the student who had asked at the end of the previous day if he could help me with papers at my desk and who had not come back to school. Then I found out from the other teachers that he had a criminal background. Teachers are not informed of their students' criminal background, which makes sense to me as many people have incorrectly assumed this or that about me based on hearsay.

I followed my colleagues' advice and declared the stolen wallet to the police, though I doubted it would help since the high incidence of such acts rendered them utterly unmanageable. Just as I had thought, it did not have any results other than further stressing me out. So I figured it might be more helpful to tell my other students about the stressful consequences for me and trust their innate goodness.

Once again, despite the other teachers' pessimism at my naivety, it worked and a few months later my wallet was found in a nearby room. The little cash that had been inside was gone but all the cards were in order. Unfortunately, by then, I had already gone through the hassle of replacing most cards, but it nonetheless felt like a victory. This was the first time, but not the last, when I experienced that if I directly explained to my students how their behavior impacted me and asked for their help, it may very well work.

On the last day of the academic year, the student I suspected, and who had not been in any of his classes since the beginning of the year (I had to give him failing grades), had to ask all of his teachers to sign out his "release" form. The purpose of this form is to make sure that all the books and material lent by the school are returned. When he came at my classroom door we stared at one another in a silence heavy with untold words. He started to blabber nervously about something else and I decided there was no point in confrontation: without a word I took the French textbook he was returning and signed his form.

There were not enough security personnel to cover the large numbers of disruptions in the school, and not once during the entire year did a security guard come to my class even though I tried calling them several times. Every day during my "free" period, I called some of my students' parents. Many never answered the phone, but amongst those who did I found that they cared deeply about their child. They often did not have the economic resources or were strapped by their jobs and did not have enough time to spend with the child, and very few parents came to their child's parent/teacher conference. It seemed to me that they often felt they had to prove their love and could thus become quite fierce. I would remember this when my son was older and his school subtly blamed me because I had been ill and unable to come immediately to the school when he was sent to a disciplinary committee. A few times, at a loss for what to do, I took up some of the school disciplinary actions, such as calling for security or completing a form that called for disciplinary actions. I quickly found out it did not result in any positive outcomes and was mostly useless. On the contrary sometimes the students became needlessly further in trouble.

This teaching job took a heavy toll on me and I further depleted my strength. That winter I had a bad case of pneumonia and I was unable to go to work for ten days. Alone in my apartment I dragged myself to the kitchen, sometimes on all fours, in order to eat or drink something. I thought the illness would go away by itself but when I completely drenched my sheets in sweat one night I realized I had to go see a doctor and I finally called my first ex-husband for help. At the doctor I was told that not coming earlier was irresponsible of me, and I was given strong antibiotics which helped me get better. When I returned to my job in school ten days later my students were surprised as they thought I had left for good.

In the spring my eyes started to itch, especially while I was using the chalk board in my classroom or when I came outside of the dark school building into the glaring outdoor light. I learned to close my eyes while erasing the chalkboard and to put on my sun glasses before stepping outside at the end of the day; but sometime I could not resist the urge to rub my itchy eyes, which I knew to be a big mistake. After a few seconds of relief, my eyes started to burn even more and I had an irrepressible urge to close them, no matter where I found myself. This happened one afternoon while I was driving home in the middle of fierce traffic and its noise. After the immediate relief, the terrible burn came and I had to close my eyes for a few seconds. It was dangerous and it scared me out of my wits, prompting me to get over my dread of doctors and go see one. Upon examining my eyes the doctor did not see anything the matter so I went to see a second doctor. The same lack of explanations occurred, the poor doctors were mystified. All they could come up with was to advise me to try over-the-counter eye drops, which I tried just to find out that it was absolutely useless. In hindsight I realized that as usual I was too stressed when at the doctor to explain myself properly. I did not make clear and self-assured statements about this eye pain and my vagueness prompted misunderstandings. I also believe that the eye itch was a reaction to stimuli during a stressful time in my life, because similar types of painful but unexplained physical reactions would happen to me again later.

My students knew I did not enforce a tough discipline and so they often acted out. I did not understand their need to act out and I took their behaviors seriously. I tried to reason with them, which was usually a complete waste of time. The only discipline rule I enforced without hesitation was that I did not stand for students hurting one another in front of me. I refused to fail them even when their attendance was irregular, and this made grading the often-absent students at the end of the semester a challenge. Just before the grades were due on the school's computer I'd beg them—sometimes I called them on the phone—to do some work so that I'd have a justification to at least give them a passing grade. During instances when I was able to meet with a student one on one I often earned their trust and respect. After all, I could identify with being different. But the respect I earned in those situations was not enough to keep the student body at large from acting out in my classroom.

At the end of the school year I was asked to leave. A German program offered to pay for a German teacher the next year and the school decided to stop offering French. I was not so sure it was necessary to cut the French program and many students appeared to really like me and to learn from me, and they needed stability. So once again I wondered what I had done wrong. Was it because I let my students play cards—with a French card deck—on the last day of school? I did not know it, but it was illegal. In any event, after only one year I once again lost the security of a stable income.

One of the most rewarding accomplishments of the year was that I met Melanie, another teacher whose friendship and support helped many times in the future. Two other positive outcomes of that year were: one, I started to do yoga every day first thing in the morning; and two, because I was so often overwhelmed with all the things I had to do, I started to write daily lists on little pieces of paper. I carried these notes everywhere in my pocket. The visualization helped me complete tasks and it also helped make them become clearer. Once I had completed a task I crossed it off the list with relish and if a task was incomplete I copied it over to the next list. Oftentimes, there came a time when I was so fed up with having to write the same thing over and over that I might finally do it, just to get rid of it on the paper!

It was really a great way to free up my mind of worry and when I lost the tiny scrawled piece of paper I was quite upset, as I often had recorded on it valuable information that was not written down anywhere else. Nowadays I still write down every reminder I can think of (they often pop up in my mind during my sitting meditation practice), but since I no longer have to spend long days at work I record them on my home desk calendar.

CHAPTER 16: TEACHING IN A SECOND SCHOOL AND ATTEMPTING STABILITY

Between my earnings, the divorce settlement money (not a huge sum, but still it helped), and the help of my French-American friend Patricia, it seemed like a good idea to attempt stability, especially when I thought about my son, Matthieu. So, I bought a two-bedroom basement apartment. This apartment seemed a good choice for many reasons. It was on a quiet dead end little street; it was not overly expansive; it was a brand new remodel; it was close to public transportation; very near lake Michigan; and it was at a walking distance from Matthieu's French school. The neighborhood on the other side of the building was somewhat infested with crime, and this new building was most likely built there in order to "better" the neighborhood, but that did not worry me so much.

When I left the rental apartment where for a year and a half I had lived as a single mother, I lost my security deposit. This struck me as unfair for several reasons: first, I left the two beautiful and sturdy shelves my designer friends had built, and, second, the only broken thing was my son's bedroom screen. Also, Patricia had helped me clean the apartment thoroughly, though it was not very dirty in the first place!) But as usual I did not think nor dare to clearly express this to the landlords at the appropriate moment, and when I thought about it I did not dare to call, time passed and then it was too late.

Because I had worked at the French school for the previous two summers, I had a little bit more income than usual and I felt rich, the most I had ever been. In order to teach tennis in the French school's gymnasium, three hours, four afternoons a week, I had to set up the heavy the poles supporting the tennis net and then put them away at the end of the day. Matthieu was about the same age as some of the other children and this was his first real exposure to group tennis lessons.

My only joy during these grim years was my little son and for him I forced myself to keep a happy front. When school began for him and it was my turn to have him stay with me for a week, a friend drove him to school in the morning and I walked to pick him up every afternoon. On our walk back home, we sang French childhood songs, for example *"l'empereur, sa femme et le petit prince"* which translates to: the emperor, his wife and the little prince.

However shortly after I had moved into the newly purchased apartment, many things went wrong with it, maybe because many kinks in the remodeled building had not been sorted out yet. A few days after I moved in, the sewer pipe just outside my bedroom backed up. I watched in anxious horror as the pipe sewer contents crept up closer and closer to my backdoor. When it stopped just short of my back door, I breathed a sigh of relief and believed it was over. But the next time it rained this happened again, though to a lesser degree, and I realized I had to call for help. This was a real hassle as it seems the building management did not really want the costly repairs to happen.

Then there were problems with the heater and the washer and dryer, for which I found somebody to fix them on my own penny. In the dead of winter the furnace broke down for good, the snow melt from the upstairs balcony leaked in my kitchen, and the quarters I kept on my dresser for the laundry disappeared. I wondered if there was a hidden message in all of this.

Since I had been let go of my first teaching job, I had been looking thoroughly for another one—at least this time I had a few months—but French teachers were not in demand and I did not interview well. None of the safer or closer high schools needed a French teacher, and the very few who needed one had many other non-autistic candidates to choose from.

At the end of the summer I once again found myself without any income source and having just bought an apartment. This constant precariousness in the state of my affairs is starting to sound like a refrain, but it unfortunately is how my non-diagnosed autistic life has often been.

I had started to look for a different job than teaching when, two weeks into the beginning of the school year, I was hired by yet another inner city high school. The French teacher who had taught there for the last several years had just had her first child and left suddenly. This second teaching job also took place in the south of Chicago, in a school not far from the previous one but in a less troubled environment. The elevated train did not go as far as the school and its neighborhood, which rendered it a sort of closed pocket left alone to its segregation. A friend later told me that when cars happened to drive by in the dark at a slow pace in this neighborhood, the people in their apartments duck down in anticipation of the stray bullets that may come.

It was another year of teaching with students' tragic stories in abundance at every turn. For many of my students, French was a subject matter miles away from their reality and it did not interest them. Quite often they did not know their own language so well and I wracked my brains to devise ways to motivate them—the previous year had given me some experience to do just that.

For example, I told them that they were beautiful young people, they were, and that they should make use of their energies, since they were at the most susceptible age for doing this. Surely they could see for themselves what became of some people who may not been able to take advantage of their schooling. They could end up stuck in poverty and uneducated in their old age, inflexible in their refusal to change.

When I walked in my classroom for the first time there was a Post-It note on the attendance roster with the words "Supreme Court" written on it. Surprised and immediately assailed by all kinds of crime-and-legality scenarios, I wondered why the court was mentioned here. I soon found out that it was only the first and last name of one of my students.

I was sometimes really impressed by my students' abilities to create distraction. Once, four or five of the most disruptive boys in the class started to tap, one on a textbook, one with a pencil, one with a coin, one with his keys: it was startling to hear the unison and rhythm they randomly produced as they worked *together*. This confirmed my suspicions that some of the most disruptive students were quite gifted.

During yet another work day, two girls in one of my afternoon classes started to fight against one another. I never knew why exactly but I was told by another teacher that an old family feud existed between them. Their long colorful nails quickly drew blood, and time slowed for me. I frantically called for security, but nobody came and due to past experiences I did not rely on their coming. I knew better than to throw myself in between them because the teacher next door did that once when two his students were fighting, and inadvertently had a tooth broken.

In despair I noticed how the other students stood by the two fighting girls and tried to talk them in stopping their fight, sometimes strategically throwing an arm or a leg in their way. This gave me an idea: I asked four responsible and strong students to work together to separate the two girls. At my count of three, two were in charge of grabbing each of the girls' arms and two others in charge of their waists. It worked rather nicely and each of the girls was pushed back on a separate chair and kept there by other students. When the security guy arrived a few minutes later he was quite surprised to find I had succeeded in breaking the fight.

My teaching ways worked for a few students; because I often had to explain a piece of French grammar and translate it into English for those who asked, many in my class improved their native-language grammar. But overall it was a losing battle; I was alone and there were too many disruptions. However the experiences of teaching in inner city high schools confirmed for me that no one is superior or inferior, and that we all deserve respect. I also found out that the African-American situation in United States is an invisible sore in many aspects. In the end teaching exhausted me and I would have recurring nightmares about it for many years after.

CHAPTER 17: CAR PROBLEMS AND AN OUT OF STATE MOVE

Matthieu and I at a Chicago airport photo booth, 1999

When the used car I bought just after my accident broke down, I had to get rid of this car too. How I now missed the good car from my former marriage that had been wrecked! Since at that time I couldn't afford to buy yet another used car, I found an alternative way to get to work just as the cold Chicago weather settled in. I lived close enough to a highway ramp that two other teachers in my school drove by there every day. Thus every workday morning I walked there, sometimes tramping through snow, and waited on a lonely dark icy stretch for one or the other of the two teachers to pick me up. At the end of the day, I walked back home from where I had been dropped off at the same spot, exhausted but still needing to pick up Matthieu at his school, which I could go walk to. At least I was able to keep going to my job on the other side of town until I could afford to buy another used car with, as always, more than one hundred thousand miles on its odometer.

It was not the end of my car problems, though the next winter there was a terrible snow storm and all schools were closed for a few days. Just before the storm, my recently acquired car broke down. Matthieu was stuck at his father's house that week. In my basement apartment, the snow piled up far on the windows, blocking out the light. Many cars in the city were immobilized by the storm for a day or two. Snow plows were much requested and there was a shortage of tow trucks. Little side streets like mine where not about to be cleared very soon, and for an entire day I could not get out of the apartment. When I finally made it outside, while climbing over piles of snow, it was an exhausting trip just to walk to the nearby store in the unbroken fresh snow.

As for my car, I had to resort to other ways to tow it. A student of my friend Patricia had his own side business and was willing to tow my car, for a little money, all the way to his place on the other side of town. A week later when the car battery was fixed and the snow mostly cleared away, I went to pick it up and brought Matthieu with me. I suspect his presence helped break the ice with the student's family. Their kindness almost had me literally tear up for gratefulness; nobody had shown me such warmth during these wretched months.

A few months later, on yet another cold winter morning, the car stalled again in the middle of a dangerous intersection while on my way to work. At least this time many teachers drove by this same place, and we were able to push the car to the nearby school parking lot. During the day, one of my students who knew about cars managed to get the car going again. However the fact that the battery was likely to break down at any time gloomily hung over me.

A few weeks later, the car died again as I was on my way back from work, but at least that time it was closer to home and I was able to park the car on the side of the road. I called the tow truck on a nearby call box and waited in the dark for over an hour, but I stayed warm inside the car. Because I absolutely needed a car I insisted that the garage find a way to fix it even though, with the shape it was in, it would not last. Finally, one evening as I was driving to a free yoga event, the car's battery died again. This time it happened in a densely forested suburb area, and there was nobody else around. It was, for me, an intense moment. I became very frightened and had a panic attack when the surrounding trees seemed to close down on me. Had it not been for the policeman who found me several hours later, I don't know that I would have ever gotten out of that forest. That was the last straw for me; I knew then that I had to change something.

I had always slept fretfully and lightly but that year this developed into full blown insomnia. I did not know what to do about it and when I finally worded my concern aloud to Patricia, she suggested I ask our doctor friend for sleeping pills. I was reluctant to do this due to their addictive capacity and because I had never in my life experienced a medicine that addressed of the root of my problem. Nevertheless, I decided to give it a try anyway, as I believed that I would have the willpower to stop. Indeed, I was so scared that sleeping pills were addictive that I stopped taking them after only a few nights though the problem did not really go away.

These various mishaps were catalysts telling me that I could not go on in the same way. It may appear to someone who never experiences such intensity that my troubles were minor, but let us remember the image of the broken door: when I am already worn out, as I was at the time, the smallest incident results in many ripples and can cause immense ravages inside me. It was extremely uncomfortable to be continuously full of anguish and not know why.

For my birthday, a friend had given me an intriguing book titled *Nothing Special/Living Zen*, by Charlotte Joko Beck. At the end of a yoga class, as I was talking about this with another student, the teacher overheard us. He then mentioned his great admiration for a Zen center near San Francisco. Coincidentally, for the upcoming Easter vacation, I was planning to visit a friend I had met online and who happened to live very near this Zen center. I was ripe for change and ready to try something new; the described practice of Zen aroused my curiosity and I decided to see if I could give it a try.

I knew from personal experience I'd better have a backup plan enabling me to earn a living and that this always took me a long time. After enquiring online, I found out that a school teacher certificated in Illinois was able to be a teacher in another state pending some requirements. In order to receive an emergency teaching credential in the state of California, I first had to pass several tests in that state. Conveniently I was able to register for a major test during the second week of my Easter vacation. For the first week, I was able to sign up as a guest student at the Zen center, and for this week I could stay at the center. It completely changed the direction of my life, for the better.

Contrary to what some of my friends had worried about, I basked into the silence of the center and I found that the daily meditation practice somehow touched something deep in me, something that I was utterly unable to explain in words. Once I was back in Chicago, and the stress and buzz of the inner city high school, it became very clear to me that I had to go back into the quiet, peaceful Zen center near San Francisco and get better acquainted with the monastic lifestyle.

The most painful part of my decision to move to a Zen center in California was my son. The thought of leaving my now seven-year-old son for a little while with his father, until I was prepared for him, was devastating. I had no intention to be without him for very long and I knew it was in my nature to follow through with what I had decided, but others did not know about my "autistic loyalty." They were worried and blamed me, and their criticisms tore me apart. Without being diagnosed in any way how could I explain that I needed to recover some strength and had to take care of myself in order to be able to care for him at a later time?

I did not have any family who could help me with Matthieu, and the only persons whom I knew really cared for him were his father and grandmother in Chicago. I disliked some of their ways, but Matthieu was no longer a baby or a toddler and at least he could now manage independently the small things such as eating and dressing. Maybe I did not trust his father and grandmother entirely, but they were basically responsible people.

Simon's reaction to my decision to move and leave Matthieu with him was negative and upsetting, which gave me great concern—but what was I to do? In order to give myself some protection in terms of legal custody matters, I wrote up a document stating that I was about to move to the San Francisco area as of August 1999 and that the visitation provisions that were indicated on the divorce decree—Matthieu would stay one week at his father and the next one with me—would therefore have to be changed." Simon reluctantly signed this document at the last minute and wrote on it: "I have received this notice and statement, but I do not agree."

Upon making the decision to move, I was immediately relieved by the idea that, with the end of the school year approaching, I would not have to worry about whether the school administration would rehire me or not for the next year. I was obviously traumatized by the past two years teaching job experiences. I had previously agreed to work another summer (the third and final one) teaching tennis at the French school, so I had another month and a half after the academic school year was over in June to dispose of my possessions before my departure to another state.

I planned to sell my apartment and use the money from the sale to pay for the move. A realtor, whom I had met at my son's school, helped me do just that. Fortunately for me, the apartment value had increased a little, and I received more money that I had expected. I saw this as another sign that I had made the right decision. The many moves in my life which were effectuated without much money and with little help had taught me that possessions can be a burden and are replaceable; I did not have enough money to move and store them in California and I yearned for a clean plate.

Consequently I sold for very little, or gave away, almost all my furniture. I was really fed up with my car so I sold it "as is" for almost nothing. I threw out many pictures, thinking that I had too many memories already cluttering my mind, and they were not always happy ones either. I only kept a few personal objects that Patricia let me store in her basement. I kept the rocking chair where Matthieu and I used to huddle up together to read, and the beautiful painting made by his kindergarten class which we had won at his school's yearly auction sale, because I hoped they would help Matthieu feel at home the day when he moved back with me. It was a difficult decision to give away Foufou the cat, whom my son and I were attached to, but at least I found some responsible people to take care of him. The friend who had bought, for a penny, my worn-out car organized a going-away party during which I was able to give Foufou to his new owners and cry, which I think was for more reasons than just losing the cat.

In August 1999 I took a plane from Chicago to San Francisco. Matthieu came with me as far as the Chicago airport and I swallowed my tears so that he would not know the gravity of the moment. The two of us had our picture taken in a tourist photo booth at the airport and for the next three years I carried that picture everywhere in my wallet. I cried during most of the plane ride. I had with me only two suitcases, one for my belongings and one for Matthieu's for the times when he would visit me. I also carried the leather briefcase my doctor friend had given me, and in which I kept all legal papers, including Matthieu's birth certificate, that would help me— and us—start a new life.

PART III

CALIFORNIA

HITTING BOTTOM BEFORE PROPER FORMAL DIAGNOSIS: 1999-2010

General Adaptation Syndrome Stage 3: Exhaustion

This is the final stage. If extended, long term damage can result. The body is at its lowest and cannot continue fighting back. It's as if the body's defensive system turns on itself for resources. The capacity of glands, especially the adrenal gland, and the immune system may be exhausted and function is impaired resulting in decompensation. The result can manifest itself in obvious illnesses such as ulcers, depression, diabetes, and trouble with the digestive system or even cardiovascular problems, along with other mental illnesses.

CHAPTER 18: SIX MONTHS AT THE ZEN CENTER FOLLOWED BY NECK AND SPINE TRAUMA

I live and work at Green Gulch Zen Center, 1999

Before going to live at the Zen center North of San Francisco as a temporary staff resident, I wanted to get to know the area a little and have Matthieu over. So for about three weeks I stayed with a friend of a friend. A week after my arrival, I bought Matthieu his first Chicago-San Francisco round trip plane ticket; there would be many more. We slept in a bedroom cottage that had neither a bathroom nor a kitchen, and in order to use these we had to cross the garden to the main house. It was a beautiful garden and since it was summer many flowers were in bloom. A few times, I found myself moved to tears to find myself in such a beautiful, peaceful spot. It felt enchanted compared to the noise and big city I had come from. The butterfly nursery fascinated Matthieu, who was about to start a new public school in Chicago. A few days after he had flown back to Chicago, I set up a rented mailbox at the nearby post office and I moved into the Zen center.

During the first six weeks of my stay at the Zen center, I slept in the dormitory for women. I shared the space with several younger women but we all were careful to be mindful of the noise we made and we only spoke in whispers. For the first month or so, the quiet of the place had an eerie feel and I sometimes got goose bumps from it. In the silence I was often able to hear the constant ringing in my ears, sometimes filled with the cries and screams of my former students. When I was assigned to my own tiny bedroom, the narrow bed and my two big bags took up the entire space; but it was quiet and private, and there was a window view of a tree. My little bedroom soon became like a palace to me.

The day started with a wake up bell at four-forty a.m. Twenty minutes later, most of the residents were in the meditation hall, or zendo, in order to start the upright-sitting practice, called zazen, where one usually sits with legs crossed and very still and quiet for forty minutes at a time. Because my diminishing energy was stronger in the morning and my body craved its wholesome benefits, I woke up twenty minutes earlier in order to be able to do my yoga routine before zazen. The days were structured in such a way that many of the Zen Center residents, including me, did a minimum of two zazen periods first thing in the morning, then worked six out of seven days until about four o'clock in the afternoon. The schedule is about the same fifteen years later. Most of the sixty residents worked on the premises; between the fields, gardens, kitchen, and guest program there was much to care for. During most of the six months I lived at this Zen Center, I worked in the guest program and many of my days started by either making a fire in a wood stove or cleaning a bathroom. On top of lodging and meals, I earned a small monthly stipend which covered the cost of my post office rental box and other small necessities.

Three times a day I ate delicious vegetarian meals and I realized then that cooking with care tremendously enhances the taste of the food. Seeing others drink plain hot water inspired me to do the same: I had always drunk much water hoping it would help my digestive system, and I found out that drinking the water hot helped. (I have a close friend who ironically calls hot water "Zen tea"). Friday was the only day in the week where a delicious dessert was cooked, and everyone on the premises made sure to be there for it.

Communication with the outside world was difficult; there was no cellular reception and the public phone booth was away from the main buildings, but there was a telephone for incoming calls very near the dining room. Matthieu could reach me there if he called exactly during mealtimes and if the phone was not busy (many people also received calls during meals, and especially at dinner). Many times, hopeful to get a call, I sat in the dining room at the table closest to the phone, jumping for nervousness each time it rang. I was only able to check my post office rental box in the nearest little town once a week or so, depending on the rides I could get on my day off.

Hoping to motivate Matthieu to learn French, I wrote my daily letters to him in my French native language and accompanied them with stickers, bubble gum and one dollar bills. But that did not work and I found out later that, though he loved the treats, he never read the letters. I scheduled my weeklong break at the same time as my son's school Thanksgiving holiday. I did not have any family or friends to stay with, so in exchange for a relatively small fee Matthieu and I were able to stay at the Zen center in one of the bigger bedrooms with bath and toilet.

Only one time during my stay did I go to watch with a few others the once-a-week movie on the sole television set available to the temporary residents. I had been told it was a quiet-type movie but after just a few minutes I felt so stressed by the noise and movement emanating from the screen that I left. Interestingly enough, this proved to be an enduring decision, as I never had a television set afterwards and I do not plan for this to change in the future.

In the back of my mind I did not forget that I might have to live outside of the Zen center someday, so during many of my days off I went to complete the tests and the other requirements for emergency-type teaching credentials in California. When I could not find a ride with one of the center's residents, I hitchhiked down the hill to the nearest town, several miles away. A French friend I had met online while looking for teaching jobs in the area came to pick me up at the nearest big intersection and drove me to a location where I could either rent a used car or take the bus.

After six months, it was time for me to go and find a way to prepare for Matthieu's return to California. I panicked at the thought of going back in a noisy and stressful environment, and of having to find a place to live and the means to support myself without any help. As a result, I had two full-blown panic attacks. As it turned out, in six months' time profound changes took place inside me. I was calmer and I became aware that I was easily overwhelmed, in a perpetual state of nervousness and hyper vigilance that was not controllable. Zen practice was the only thing that made sense to me, even if, paradoxically, it did not really make sense of anything and was so very difficult at times. Because explaining Zen with words seems to me impossible and useless, I especially liked a recipe analogy I once heard: we can learn it and its ingredients by heart but until we actually do it we do not really know it.

In each of the apartments I moved in and out of after this experience, I set up a simple little altar with a broken Buddha statue, the altar cloth and the zafu (a black, round cushion) that were given to me by friends at the Zen center. The amount of time I sat zazen steadily increased over the years. For a long time I was unaware of some of the deeper changes, but overtime I realized that the Zen practice subtly and radically transformed my life. I have real reasons to doubt that I would be alive today without it, and I was extremely fortunate to have stumbled upon this practice.

Three weeks after I had left the Zen center, at the beginning of February 2000, an intense pain in my neck and spine woke me up in the middle of the night—an occasion which I will later refer to as "The Night". I crawled to the bathroom in the hope to be able to get rid of the awful nausea but this did not happen and, since I had exhausted all my strength, I stayed on the bathroom floor for several hours. When I had enough strength to crawl back to my bed a few hours later I lay there completely still so as not to worsen the pain. When daylight finally broke I found that I was able to stand up and walk but it was extremely painful and slow. I could not twist my neck in any way on the left side. Instead, I turned to the left with my legs rather than the spine. It took another three months before I was able to turn my neck to the left despite the painful and tense sensation.

During these months driving and other daily chores were very difficult, but I could not afford to stop working and I did not have any medical insurance. The condition festered away unattended. Once I saw a chiropractor, and another time an acupuncturist, but these were like mere drops of water in the ocean. For many years afterward I wondered why this trauma happened. The major difference in my life from before The Night when my neck seized up was that I had just come out of the Zen center, back into the noisy environment of urban life. May this have been a precipitating reason? Perhaps the condition was a result of the despair I felt at the idea of leaving the stress-free haven I had found at the Zen center and the tension of entering the "outside world"?

When my body reorganized itself in this way, I was sharing an apartment in Marin County while I worked as a substitute teacher in middle and high schools in the area. After I left Zen center, my California emergency teaching credential allowed me to substitute teach in public schools. I taught many subjects, from English to Science, however there were not so many assignments in French. If the subject matter to teach was beyond me (i.e. a high school physics class), I found a student who seemed to know the subject well and be responsible, and I asked her or him to help me. They were always happy to oblige and often interested their classmates, as evidenced by the many subject-oriented questions asked.

Marin County schools were a far cry from the Chicago inner-city schools I had experienced. The schools were wealthier and smaller, the physical surroundings, often natural, were quieter and more peaceful, and the weather was often warm and sunny. One morning on a sunny spring day the entire student body of the elementary school I worked at gathered outside near the playground to watch an acrobatic show for bicycles. A huge angled ramp had been set up for the professionals on their bicycles to jump on and fly through the air, and the children's delight was obvious. Thinking of how much my son would have enjoyed this show, I started to cry behind my sun glasses and I vowed to myself that I would bring him someday in a similar school environment. I had to find a way to live with him in this affluent county!

Every penny I made that was not used for paying my rent or other necessities, I saved for plane tickets so Matthieu could come and visit me during his school breaks. At Easter that year he came for what was now his third visit to California. This time, for a week, we shared my mattress on the floor. I tried to do fun and interesting things with him: we went to the beach, visited Alcatraz (a rocky island in the middle of the San Francisco bay, famous as the site of a now defunct federal penitentiary), and played tennis together. I borrowed a friend's tent so we could camp at the nearby Taylor park, famous for its sequoias, but there was a storm and the ground was so soaked that the tent's stakes would not stay and we had to turn back.

Meanwhile my roommate became very uncomfortable with me, and, as usually, I just could not understand why as nothing practical had been wrong between us. I was always clean and quiet in order to compensate—for what I did not know exactly. So often people who had at first been delighted to live with me seemed after a while to become uncomfortable with me. The mood between us turned sour for reasons I could not decipher. Since it felt to me like she wanted me out, even though she never really put it in these exact words, I soon left. In any case, I had to go back to a university in order to fulfill the requirement for a clear teaching credential and the cheapest way to do this was to move to San Francisco.

CHAPTER 19: SAN FRANCISCO HOUSING CHALLENGES AND CHILDLESSNESS

In San Francisco, I first moved in the spare bedroom of an older woman who had become a widow not long ago. I stayed a lot in my bedroom, either studying or, in the mornings, doing yoga and zazen in front of my altar. I also did this in order to avoid the hub of stimuli such as noises and movements, and because experience had shown me that I somehow ended up making others so uncomfortable that they resented me. But despite my best efforts—or maybe because of them—my landlord soon was unhappy with me. She said that I was anti-social and that she would rather have male energy around. Vulnerable, I blamed myself and less than a month after I had moved in, I moved out again.

Just like I had concluded in Chicago ten years ago, I decided I'd probably do much better living alone, if only I could find a very cheap way to do so. Thus I rented a furnished little room off the garage of a house in a mostly Asian San Francisco neighborhood. Only a plywood wall separated me from the owners' cars and I had to cross the garage in order to go to the toilet or to the laundry room, in which an electric hot plate and a microwave were set up. But I was by myself, I had my own entrance door near the garage, and I was able to set up my altar on the commode.

Just as I had thought it might, this arrangement worked well. The Chinese owners greatly appreciated the quiet, unobtrusive ways I had honed. The few times our paths crossed were not enough for them to pass judgment or find my behavior disturbing. Down in the garage, I was mostly out of their sight and in their eyes I was the perfect renter.

Unfortunately this arrangement was really not suitable for a young child. When nine-year-old Matthieu visited me, we had to share the bed and he could not take a shower. In the middle of the night I had to go with him in order to cross the garage to go to the bathroom. One night he left his gum on the dresser and the next morning there was a trail of ants.

Luckily, during these years I was able to spend summers with Matthieu at Patricia's who, once again, came to my rescue. For two summers I stayed with Matthieu at her big house in a suburb on the North of Chicago. There, Matthieu and I had our own bedroom with two single beds and a bathroom. Every weekday I had to take Matthieu to his summer camp located about fifteen miles from Patricia' house. I did not have a car so we often took the bus and rode our bikes, which was a challenge since Matthieu was so young and the stimuli in noisy and crowded places increasingly gave me migraines and nausea. Despite her family's opposition, Patricia sometimes lent us her car and she also paid for our food and helped with clothes and some of the items I urgently needed.

Back in my garage-bedroom, whenever the owner's daughter started her car's engine, the exhaust fumes that seeped through the door gave me terrible headaches and nausea, and these health concerns and the care of Matthieu prompted me to move again.

Finding housing seems too often be a major challenge for many autistic people. If we are able to find housing independently of our parents, we often have to watch every penny. After some time our different ways may strain our relationships with the people around us. The usual explanation for this is to say that it is due to the odd behaviors resulting from our hypersensitivities or lack of "normal social" ways. I also wonder at times if our vulnerability might not be yet another cause for discomfort, as it directly reaches out to the other person's vulnerability, of which she or he may be completely unaware.

Eventually, the atmosphere surrounding us may be felt by our extraordinarily sensitive nervous system to be so intense that we no longer can stand it. We may not defend ourselves and at the least show of disapproval, we move away in a hurry—at least that is how it was for me and I have heard similar stories from other autistic individuals. I think of myself as fortunate to have had the freedom to move to a country that better allowed for differences, but I was always financially stressed, and finding the kind of environment I needed was an exhausting struggle.

The student loan I received was not enough to be able to live in the city and have Matthieu visit me during his school vacations so I kept substitute teaching. Just like what I had known in Chicago, San Francisco schools were often filled with poverty and violence, and the substitute teacher was an easy target for the students. Though I did my best to ignore it, the spasms in my neck increased. With the constant nagging of dull pain in my back my vulnerability was immediately detected by many of my students. In my eyes it seemed obvious that city life often negatively affected its inhabitants, and substitute teaching in San Francisco made that very clear.

In a perfect parallel with the chronic pain in the left side of my neck, my sensory thresholds kept lowering. Although I may appear collected even today, like churning waters below a still surface, I am extraordinarily vulnerable to stress. Because of this, I often question if the person next to me who appears very happy is really so. In reality, he or she might be extremely unhappy. Also, I often figure out ways to ease matters as much as possible, to take as much care of myself as is possible within my limited means.

Just before I was to leave the Zen center, I had half-heartedly signed up for the email list of a nearby Zen Buddhist group, or sangha, that was about to start. Generally, if I am invited somewhere I am very likely to accept the invitation whether it is good for me or not. In this case though, it was a good thing. When I was notified by mail of this sangha's one day meditation retreats, I made it a point to attend. I had little money but the sangha always gave me a scholarship and I somehow managed the strength to do a one-day retreat approximately every six months.

A few times while sitting zazen I felt faint. A feeling of extreme warmth overcame me and before it reached my heart, I quietly and slowly moved my knees up so I could rest my head down and wait for it to pass, hoping I would not keel over. I kept at it because despite its challenges zazen brought me an unexpected clarity. For example, as a strong safeguard against suicidal thoughts, I came to the realization that taking away this precious life of mine would be extremely painful to others—of that I was sure!

The few times I saw doctors at the neighborhood traditional health clinic for unexplainable symptoms, like my many reactions to stimuli, they did not have the resources to suspect autism. I not-so-assertively dropped hints about the pain in my neck, but the clinic was over-crowded and the doctors did not have enough time to pay attention. In retrospect I realized that I was not at all what they expected about autism; not only did I speak fluently in another language, I also had a child. I wondered if seeing a counselor would help. As I found out when I looked for such help, San Francisco offers a wide range of low-income services. During my first two years in the city I saw three young counselors who had a sliding scale, but none of them came close to understanding me. They were well-meaning but my challenges were beyond them. Without having a clue as to what I was referring to, I often said to these counselors that I was the best actress. I felt like a sick tree whose roots, where the real problem lay, were not seen.

CHAPTER 20: UNIVERSITY AND LAST FULL-TIME JOB

San Francisco State University best student loan rate required me to study for a Master's degree. So, on top of classes I needed in order to obtain a California clear teaching credential, I studied for a French Master's. I also added physical education to my credential in order to increase job possibilities. The classes required for future teachers often seemed tedious. Though a few of the teachers were interesting, many of them seemed to only stress the conformity of future teachers.

I did my best to not be highly visible and I always completed my homework on time and as completely as possible. But in many classes I sat in the back, which apparently led one teacher to assume I was unengaged. I don't know exactly what this teacher assumed, but she must have been seriously displeased, though I had no clue about it. Stunned, I received a failing grade, my first ever in United States. I had turned in all the work on time and had had decent grades on it, so I dared appealing in writing to the higher authorities in that department and the failing grade was quickly taken off my records. I am often better able to make an argument to defend myself in writing.

The classes in the Physical Education subjects were sometimes more interesting. Once I had to take a tennis class but there was no advance level class available, so I took the intermediate level class. The good news was that I could manage it while playing only with my non-dominant hand so as not to use the side of my neck and shoulder that was painful. The only time I used my dominant hand was when I felt it was necessary to win my serve. But when the teacher noticed my skill, she asked me to demonstrate the serve movement to my classmates. Instead of saying I could not,

I obliged and, even worse, I felt compelled to demonstrate my best in front of the other students. Naturally this sent a sharp pain down my shoulder and by the second time around, I was unable to repeat the motion. I had no formal explanation for this pain and I did not know how to explain it. The teacher was disappointed and probably assumed, like most everyone else, that it would soon pass.

When I finished the university classes for teaching, I became legally able to teach at a California public high school. I had not yet completed my Masters in French so I kept taking classes for it even while I worked full-time. French classes were the best part of the university experience. I enjoyed reading again books I had been too young and inexperienced to understand in my youth. Also, I had the advantage of being a native and others often asked for my help. For example, when I re-read *Pantagruel* by Francois Rabelais, I revisited a famous story that had always intrigued me and suddenly I understood better something about me. In the book, the character Panurge throws the lead sheep of a herd off a boat, and all the sheep in the herd follow behind it and jump to a certain death. Until then I had believed I did the opposite of blindly following a leader but, in fact, my entire life I often was, and still am, easily pushed around by whoever is around me at the time.

I remember two other meaningful university experiences. In one of them I could not afford the university parking fees, so each time I had to come to a class I circled the streets in search of an available spot. This could take up to an hour as other students did the same and at times it felt like a cut throat business. It often left me slightly nauseous or with a fast beating heart. The second peripheral but meaningful experience was the question of showers. In the garage, where my bedroom was, there was no shower stall, so once a week I tiptoed unnoticed in the university's physical education building to wash my shoulder-length, thick, curly hair. I was registered there, but I was embarrassed and did not want to have to explain myself. I suspect that, as has so often been the case in my life, I looked as if I had something to hide. Fortunately for me, in this instance it did not matter. The anonymity of being one student in the midst of many was helpful. But during holidays and breaks, the university was closed, so I was unable to wash my hair for up to two weeks. On Melanie's advice, I bought a shower-faucet spray attachment and washed my hair a few times in my little sink, though it was difficult.

The final work necessary for a Masters in French was mostly in writing, which was helpful for me as it was less socially demanding that way. Despite the many adversities I received my Masters in January 2004.

With my previous inner city school experience I was able to find a job, teaching both physical education and French classes, in a San Francisco high school. My office was in the girl's locker room under the school's gymnasium. There was a shower stall in it and at the beginning of the school year I still lived in the garage-side bedroom without a shower. I scrubbed the school's shower stall so that I would be able to take showers before it was time to open the locker room to the students. It was so unheard of for a teacher to do this at school that, once, three students stormed past me to check out for themselves if it was true that I did use the shower stall.

My hypersensitivities pervaded my life and often prompted a behavior that did not make sense to others. In order to avoid unpleasant stimuli when I did not have classes, I stayed in my office. At the beginning of the school year I bought a coffee dispenser to boil hot water, and there, every day, I ate the lunch I had brought from home. In order to make my office a sort of refuge, with a friend's help I brought down an easy chair that had been discarded. Every few precious minutes I had to myself, I relaxed on the chair with a cup of hot water, colorful earplugs and the light turned off. Many colleagues and students thought that I purposely was not "social."

On September 11, 2001, the United States declared a state of national emergency after the terrorist attacks, and all of the nation's public schools shut down. If my friend, the other P.E teacher, had not come down to my office to warn me, I would not have known it and might have been locked in the building.

When the students were in the locker room, the smell of their fragrances made me gag. I just could not believe the acuity with which stimuli impacted me, it was so unheard of! Ironically, a few times being so sensitive to smells had its reward: when students smoked marijuana, I smelled it immediately and the amazed students wondered how I knew, while covering their mouth with their T-Shirts.

When a student slashed me with her key chain and left a mark on my neck, I dared to tell the school's principal. But I declined to pursue the matter further, telling the principal that I felt that the French saying "dirty laundry is washed within the family" was true. In truth, here again, I did not know how to assert myself and I paid for it dearly. After this incident, I became this student's whipping boy. Several times she stuck out her leg when I walked by her desk hoping that I would trip on it (but I had an "autistic eye" for detecting movement). Another time she put some kind of glue on the phone mouthpiece in the classroom where I taught; some other student rang the phone during class, but another teacher happened to be in the room at that exact moment, and when she went to answer it, the student asked her not to answer, and had to explain what she had done. A few months later, in a conference with this student's parents and the school's vice-principal, her parents were somewhat verbally abusive and the vice-principal did not say a word in my defense. Another teacher told me later that these parents both had powerful positions in the San Francisco school administration.

CHAPTER 21: GETTING READY FOR MY SON AND AN ODYSSEY

While working full-time and going to the university part-time I also juggled preparations for Matthieu to come and live with me, motivated by my love for him and the certainty that it was most important for a young child to be reunited with his mother. About three months after I started teaching, I was finally able to afford to move in a bigger space, with a roommate of course. The basement apartment I rented was only three blocks away but it had two bedrooms, a kitchen and a bathroom with a shower. I warned my roommate before she moved in with me that she would have to leave sometime in the spring as I was planning for my son's return during the next summer.

When I told Simon that I planned to bring Matthieu to live with me, he was not so supportive. He made what sounded to me like threats to keep Matthieu with him, and they scared me so much that I felt forced to legally request the change in Matthieu's living arrangement. This had to be done in a Chicago court because the divorce decree had been executed there. I sensed that sometimes I was rather unable to articulate myself so well. Consequently, without any advice from others, I carefully put together a big fat file as a form of defense. In it I painstakingly detailed the history of Matthieu and my separation and the many steps I had taken to be reunited with him. In an attempt to assuage my anxieties, I copied the file twice. But it turned out to be of no use whatsoever; as soon as the judge asked Simon to make a statement, he declared that he had "no intention to rescind the agreement." This was a reference to the agreement that we had both signed back when I was about to move to California, and it also meant that he agreed to let Matthieu come and live with me in San Francisco. This courtroom declaration was so important to me that it stayed forever carved in my memory.

Since I was now working full-time for the first time since my arrival in California, I had health insurance. Thus, when a spasm intensified the pain in my neck, I took a chance and went to the nearby hospital emergency room. I could not take a cab since I could not take the chance of being exposed to the taxi driver's potential loud radio or perfume without my neck tensing, so I had to drive myself. It was a dangerous feat since I could not at all turn my neck to the left but I'd rather dare this than risk a potential increase in the pain. At least it was during the night so there was not much traffic.

The doctor who saw me that night only gave me a muscle relaxant and a prescription for pain killers which did nothing to address the root of the problem. In the next few days the spasm in my neck relaxed enough that I could resume work, but the painful tension was still there underneath.

After a hard day's work at school, I was lying exhausted on my bed one afternoon when my ingrained belief that it was completely useless and counterproductive to ask the medical people for help was suddenly shaken. In that moment it dawned on me that I could not be the only one on earth to feel like this, and I could no longer believe that the discomfort and pain I experienced were only in my imagination. I had no other choice than to try to figure it out. I asked for a thorough check up at the nearby hospital and naturally the usual pattern occurred: I was unable to adequately explain myself and after one brief visit the doctor seemed to have decided it was all in my head. When I received the results of the tests in the mail, she had handwritten on them "excellent cholesterol," which was not at all relevant to my pain.

At the end of the year, my contract as a full-time teacher was not renewed. The day the assistant principal (the one who had earlier chosen not to defend me) told me that I was not being rehired, I cried and asked why, but no answer was offered. My usual curse of being easily overwhelmed disabled me so much that I was unable to tell him the reason why I was so crushed: I had to be able to support my soon-to-be-returned son, and how would I do this if I did not have a job?

During the summer I planned to pick up Matthieu in Chicago and drive a rented truck back to San Francisco with him, his belongings and the stuff I had left in storage in Patricia's basement three years earlier. I was unable to fly, both because my hypersensitivities were increased around people and because I did not have the money for it. It would be easier to drive the approximate two-thousand miles alone with my son. The trip would become an odyssey.

I had booked the Chicago rental moving truck by phone from San Francisco, but when I called the truck company from Patricia's house in order to confirm it, I was told that no truck was available. I was devastated, as all my plans depended on us getting in a timely manner to San Francisco. Hearing my despair, Patricia's wealthy husband called and threatened the moving truck company with a law suit. It worked, they found a truck for me and I loaded it, with Matthieu's parakeet in its cage safely tucked between us in the cab.

The drive lasted four days; it would have been only three days if the truck had not needed repairs. It had been steadily slowing down since we had left Chicago. I could feel there was a problem but I wanted to believe that the truck would make it. Two times during the first half of the trip I had the engine checked out; but the truck company repair men did not find anything wrong and appeared to believe I made a fuss over nothing. However as Matthieu and I were about to go through the salt flats of Bonneville, west of Salt Lake City, the truck was going slower and slower and with miles of desert before us, I realized that this was dangerous. I just could not safely press on.

Sobbing desperately, I called the rental company again and this time the repair man asked me to return to Salt Lake City for the repair; they would put us up in a hotel for the night. Driving back took us another hour in scorching heat, with the heater on to keep the engine cooler. It turned out that a screw on the fan belt was loose, and we were able to start again the next day.

My son's long lasting memory of that trip would be the time when, in the hotel, I smelled something foul and frantically went to look everywhere for the reason. When I finally got around to smelling my own stinky socks, I screamed and ran for the shower. My own memorable moment was of the time when we missed the correct turn because we were arguing over the music on the radio. We ended up going back in the direction we had just come out from: the salt desert. There was not exit for another forty miles and I did not want to drive another eighty miles back and forth. I took a good look at the ten yards of white substance that divided the two freeways lanes and drove through it. I prayed that the wheels not get stuck and my son was afraid that the earth would open under us. But we made it, and when I returned the truck in San Francisco, the moving truck rental company staff was surprised to see white salt on all the wheels.

Since I had brought my son's birth certificate with me, I was able to register him in a San Francisco elementary school without a fuss. Matthieu was entering fifth grade. The school was only a few relatively safe blocks from our apartment so he could walk back and forth by himself. I found a family therapy center that scaled fees according to income because I felt it would be really helpful for Matthieu with the transition to a new city,

Once Matthieu started school, I started to work once again as a substitute teacher in the city. I was called in every morning with an offer for work that day, but my inordinate hypersensitivities made it difficult. Each time I had to find the designated school, park in a city where parking is notoriously difficult, and deal with strangers, both staff and students. At least I was able to choose the days whether I would work or not except that I did not make any money on the days I did not work—no small matter for me.

When I turned down the day's assignment, it was almost always because I was overwhelmed by fatigue, which was increasingly frequent.

Matthieu saw his counselor once a week and I could see that he was happy about it and that it helped him. Whereas he had often been in trouble at his Chicago school, during his two years in San Francisco he did not get in trouble once. He was also able to participate in a rock climbing therapeutic activity, which fostered in him a love of rock climbing.

Matthieu must have explained our household financial difficulties to his counselor, because once a week she started to take me to various vegetarian restaurants. Even though I am no longer in touch with her, I am indebted to her for this. It is amazing how hunger creates solid bonds. I suspect that anybody who has ever been hungry knows exactly what I am speaking about here.

The neighborhood afterschool activities where I signed Matthieu up were not always successful. Matthieu's bike was stolen and he had several fights with other children. So, instead, I enrolled him in another low-income program specifically meant to enrich inner city kids' lives through learning to play tennis with real professionals. A perk of living in the city of San Francisco is that there were many opportunities for people like us without much money. I had difficult affording Matthieu's first tennis racket, but his upset father refused to help me with anything at that time.

I could not drive in the dark any longer, the many lights (especially headlights) blinded and gave me migraines and nausea. So I drove Matthieu to his tennis lessons while it was still daylight but he had to take the bus back home afterwards, and each time I was very worried. It may have been only one bus ride, but it lasted forty minutes and went through neighborhoods that were not always so safe. This was before cell phones existed, so I had Matthieu call me from a pre-agreed-upon payphone exactly when he left and I calculated his estimated arrival time. When he did not arrive on time several times, I became so anxious that I called the bus company, but it never got me anywhere and Matthieu always showed up while I was fretting. Since I worked less, I started to play tennis more often with Matthieu, using my non-dominant hand in order to avoid tensing my painful left side.

I tried to visit children-friendly places with him, like the Lawrence Hall of Science in Berkeley and the Santa Cruz board walk. Each time it drained me, I had pounding migraines, dizziness, tinnitus, the muscles in my left leg twitched, and I could not sleep for a few nights afterward. Soon enough, lack of money was also an excuse not to go to big stores and other loud busy places.

CHAPTER 22: SURVIVING WITH MATTHIEU AND MOVING AGAIN

A few months after Matthieu came back, it became clear that I was heading toward financial disaster. Substitute teaching and the student loan were not enough for the two of us to live on. I had started to skip on my own diet so Matthieu would have something to eat, and several times I had longingly looked at the people eating inside restaurants.

Since I did not work full-time, neither Matthieu nor I had health insurance. Spurred by the energy of despair, I decided to go and ask for public assistance at the San Francisco Department of Health and Human Services. Each of the several visits to the HHS meant long waits in overcrowded lines and unsupportive staff. By the time I met with someone in charge, I was a wreck and unable to articulate myself. Several times I got the impression that they believed me to be a spoiled white person making my needs up. However, I gritted my teeth and persevered as it allowed Matthieu and me to have minimum medical coverage and food stamps.

Sometimes I don't think that the HHS counselor who met with me realized I was an immigrant. When I checked the "Caucasian" category on documents, this did not explain that I was a first generation immigrant and several times it was assumed that I was born and raised in United States, or that since I was from a wealthy country it followed that I, myself, was wealthy.

One of HHS requirements was that, as a single mother, I register with the San Francisco Child Support Agency. This was one of those moments where I sensed that something dramatic would result. I remember calling my sister in Canada from a public phone during a rain storm, crying hysterically. Several months later I found out that Simon had been asked by the state of California to give his financial support, and it terribly angered him. He once again threatened to keep Matthieu at his next vacation with him, and he further withdrew his already scant support, so I did my best to let the matter drop with the San Francisco Child Support Agency.

At the same time I registered with the San Francisco Housing Authority, and less than a year later, I was offered an apartment in the city's low income public housing. On a bright Sunday morning, Matthieu and I drove around the public housing, and I realized with horror how life-threatening the place would probably be for Matthieu and me, even if financially it was an unparalleled offer. My two African-American friends also had the sense to discourage me further.

I was now a little bit older and more careful about my choice of a sex partner. I also thought that maybe if the man was not always there, it might be better, both for me and for Matthieu. Thus, I met a sweet man who was not truly available, and I found out that I did not like this uncommitted relationship either. In an attempt to stop myself from entering into shallow intimacy, I wrote myself a note in red ink and stuck the piece of paper to the front of my desk. It said that from now on, I would only enter into a committed long-term relationship. I kept this note pinned to my desk cork board for about five years. I only discarded it once I became so withdrawn in my nameless illness that I no longer felt "at risk."

One day while I was substitute teaching in an inner city high school, I fainted. The overpowering smell of cleaning agent in one of the class-rooms, that I was in for just a few seconds, caused such a drop in my blood pressure that when I stood up suddenly several hours later, I passed out. The paramedics were called, and my first thought upon coming to a few minutes later was that I did not have the money to pay for them. When I saw the doctor a few days later, my telling about the offensive smell was dismissed per usual and a "vase-vagal" diagnosis was made. (This is a drop on blood pressure caused by an overactive vagus nerve.)

A little, hushed voice inside me warned me that I'd better move us out of the city while I still had enough energy for it. I had never forgotten my vow to bring my son to the sunnier, wealthier and safer public schools in Marin County. Once I completed my Master's degree and Matthieu finished sixth grade, I used the extra income I had earned thanks to a gig working online for a French textbook company for three months, and I rented a truck and moved us out of San Francisco.

I wanted a place that was as far away as possible from noise and city bedlam, while still within easy reach of food supplies and in close proximity to a bus line. While searching, I found out that without money, staying away from noise is extremely difficult as the cheaper apartments are nearly always located near a noise source.

I asked the Housing Authority if I could get any help, but when I visited the shared community housing they offered, I found out it meant that Matthieu and I would have to share the same bedroom, and that there would be people (and noise and all other sensory overload) in the remainder of the house. I came to the difficult conclusion that even if I really could only barely afford the rent, I must make it a priority to live alone with Matthieu. To the staff at the Housing Authority it looked as if I were picky.

The one-bedroom apartment I finally rented was in a complex with about thirty other apartments. I shared a wall with three other apartments and I could hear the nearby boulevard traffic through the windows, but it was surrounded by hills and the view from any of my windows was about half-filled with the green of trees. The weather was mild and sunny, and Matthieu's middle school, the bus line, grocery stores and the public library were all within walking distance.

A friend helped us move in exchange for his use of the rented truck on that day. I had to plan carefully where we set down the furniture in our new apartment, as I correctly assessed that I would be too weak to move it again later. In order to give Matthieu some independence, I gave him the bedroom while I put my bed in a corner of the living room. I immediately set up an altar in a corner in order to be able to do my daily sitting meditation.

In order to keep minimal health insurance and food stamps, I registered with Marin county Department of Health and Human Services. This county's HHS was a lot more supportive. On top of my previous benefits, I was allotted much-needed monthly financial help and I was enrolled in CalWORKS (California Work Opportunity and Responsibility to Kids).

Another priority was to find a medical clinic. Our health insurance limited us to traditional medical clinics but I tried to find a progressive one that was located in a quiet location. A friend recommended one that was mainly accessible by car only. The distance to get to it was a little daunting, but I felt it was more important for me to be away from the all-encompassing noise.

During my first visit, I broke down and told Dr. H. that I felt like a candle at the end of its wick. When I mentioned how sounds, smells and lights gave me migraines and other ailments, Dr. H. told me to stay away from them. I cringed while thinking how impossible this was given that these were all around me. Since when I am rushed my challenges to communicate increase, I was not able to further explain this to the doctor, nor was I able to mention the pain in my neck and the inordinate drinking of one gallon of hot water a day. That first day, Dr. H. referred me for psychotherapy and I was assigned a French therapist, which made me feel grateful, as if the county was paying attention to its poorer inhabitants.

At first I was reticent and not forthcoming with the French therapist, but soon I saw that she was open to different ways. She listened, realized that I needed medical attention and for the next three years advocated for me. When no answer to her phone calls and emails about me arrived from the traditional medical clinic, she drove the forty miles round trip, only to be told that my doctor was unavailable—all this was quite frustrating for her.

That winter, for the third time in a row, I wheezed and coughed heavily. The bouts left me exhausted and my lungs burned. At least the wheezing and coughing symptoms were easily noticeable, and the doctor immediately declared it to be asthma and said it would return. However, the next winter the symptoms did not appear and they never returned again afterward. I believe this improvement was due to the new and less stressful environment I lived in. Instead of humid city basement apartments and exposure to a fairly large city's pollution, I was now surrounded by sun and nature.

CHAPTER 23: EXHAUSTED AND PARALYZED

At first, I had a car and I still had enough energy to be able to drive around. Being in a quieter and sunny environment boosted my energy levels and I join a few social activities. Besides my regular sitting meditation sessions alone at home, I joined a new Zen Buddhist sangha that met once a week and for a couple of hours in the evening. Once again I tried to play competitive tennis. Though I found a way to win several matches by registering in a lower-level category, I was too exhausted and stressed out to do this ever again. I also traded cleaning for yoga lessons at the nearby studio that I biked to. I was able to clean while alone and with a natural citrus-smelling window cleaner, which did not give me migraines.

But ever so slowly, the world shrank around me. I was becoming more and more unable to withstand any stimuli and these hypersensitivities put a heavy damper on all of my activities. For fear of the painful effects (neck and spine spasms, migraines, dizziness, fatigue, etc.) caused by any form of stimulus, I did my best not to go out and this was often misinterpreted.

Because I could not afford to be choosy, I added elementary grades and special education classes to my substitute teacher card, which previously was only registered for middle and high schools. Often the students seemed to like me, but I did not always do so well with the other teachers. For example, it sometimes happened that an autistic student in a special education class did not overact at my sudden presence with him or her, and stayed with me longer than they did with some other adults that they had known longer. One teacher complained that I refused to carry around a handicapped child. At the time, it was surprising but in hindsight, of course, it makes sense since I myself am autistic, and I had this terrible, nameless pain in my neck, shoulder and back.

When my car required a repair job that was too expensive for my means, I got rid of it and stopped driving altogether; it was too overwhelming sensory-wise. At first I still managed to take the bus or go by bike to substitute teach in a few nearby schools.

In order to get to the traditional medical clinic, I hitchhiked on the nearby boulevard, which went over many hills in the country side and was therefore safer for me. Or I borrowed the car of a friend. As a last resource I took the shuttle service, but between the limited bus schedule, the poor suspension on a bumpy road, and riders with fragrances, it was so challenging that I'd rather take a chance and hitch a car ride.

In order to supplement my small income I found several part time jobs that I could get to by bike. Once a week, I went to a Lutheran church in order to teach Sunday school. Later, I biked once a fortnight for an overnight at the house of an older lady I helped take care of, and eventually I translated French emails for an independent small business.

But my decreasing ability to work, and the HHS monthly financial help, was not enough to cover our monthly expenses. While I still had the strength to advocate some for myself, I signed up for all the help I could get with other agencies. One organization paid for half of my monthly rent several times and another one obtained for me the quality cooking pots I had asked for as a Christmas wish.

I calculated how much each day's rent cost and was careful of each and every of the necessities I bought. The money I received every month from public assistance allowed me to pay for almost half of the rent. Food stamps and Matthieu's free school lunch covered our food, which included lots of bread and pasta. The remaining portion I had to earn somehow, so when I could no longer work it was terrifying.

I could not avoid taking the shuttle bus in order to go to a mandatory meeting with CalWORKS. But the noise of the shuttle bus radio, combined with the bright lights and movement in the waiting room, so overwhelmed me that I passed out in front of the case worker. It turned out that this was a blessing in disguise: it dispelled the belief that I was faking my discomfort and the CalWORKS staff came to my help. One way in which they helped was that for the next two or three years I was assigned a case worker to drive me back and forth to various medical appointments.

The year 2006 turned out to be the eve of the paralysis in the left side of my neck and shoulder, when I became severely incapacitated. It was fortunate that my current Zen teacher gave me two supportive emotional anchors just before the paralysis happened.

First were the meetings. Once a week, and for an entire year, I had hourly meetings one-on-one with him (these are sometimes called "doku-san" in Zen parlay). I was able to do this because we met during the day. I only had to bike two flat blocks in order to get there and he allowed me to only pay a token few dollars each time. When he found out how ill I was, he offered to go with me and see my doctor but I turned down the offer since I did not see how my problems could be rapidly resolved. Also, he was not as available as he had been previously—a few months later he became the Abbott of the San Francisco Zen center.

My meetings with him had another helpful result. In July 2006, he gave me Jukai, a Zen lay ordination ceremony where one makes a vow to respect as much as possible simple precepts like not killing, stealing, lying and so forth. In the months preceding this ceremony I had stitched together, with much help from expert sangha members, a rokasu, which is a delicately constructed bib representing Buddha's robe.

At the same time, because I desperately wanted to appear "normal" and also rather childishly, I kept doing things that were not at all good for me. Despite the fact that it stimulated the pain in my neck and back, the next summer I stayed for a few weeks at Patricia's in Chicago. Not only did I stay there for free, I could see Matthieu who, now that he lived with me, visited his father during every school vacation. Finally I was able to visit former friends. The summer of 2006 was a particular stressful visit, and I had a raging argument with a friend. On the day of my departure, it was with great difficulty, stopping every few steps, that I carried my luggage up and down the public elevated train that took me to the airport. My neck hurt so much I no longer cared what other people thought and I cried in public, a rare event.

One week after my return home, early in the month of September, the painful cramping in my neck that I had managed to repress for the past six years caught up with me. One morning, like a bottle exploding from too much pressure, the knot in my neck clenched with rock-like solidity and I found myself moaning on the floor of my apartment.

Despite feeling as if I had been branded by a hot iron, after a few hours I slowly brought myself up to a standing position, only to find out that the left side of my neck was paralyzed, with the pain radiating to my shoulder and down the spine. I was unable to put any weight on my left foot and when I pushed my arm up with the other hand it did not go up more than one or two inches. It was as if a tight rubber band was knotted in the side of my neck and several nerves had been pinched.

The next day was a Sunday and I was expected to teach Sunday school. I could not cancel it since I had already cancelled the three weeks before in order to go to Chicago. Though I feared that my neck would snap and no longer support my head, I dug my son's old crutches from his closet and limped across the street to the church. When he saw me and my crutches, one of the church-goers took pity and offered to drive me the next morning to the traditional medical clinic.

At the clinic that morning, Dr. H. was the only doctor available for an emergency visit. During my initial visit to the clinic, Dr. H. had been the one to refer me to psychotherapy. However, I now saw another doctor at that clinic, since Dr. H. had already decided that I was making my symptoms up and that I was exaggerating my pain. Even though I indicated a "9" on the rather infamous pain scale of zero to 10, Dr. H. did not look very far into my pain. I was too overwhelmed with pain to be able to advocate for myself and I did not realize how poorly the doctor thought of me. I liked him well enough and I was unable to imagine his misunderstandings. After all, he had previously given Matthieu his old climbing shoes. The common pain killers he prescribed did not touch the pain.

Back at home, I found that the slightest pressure applied on some parts of my body sent an electric current of pain down my spine. Also, the pain in my neck made my already light sleep almost completely impossible. For the entire first week, two hours before going to bed, I alternated the uncomfortable ice pack made of ice cubes from my freezer and the old fashion hot water bottle. I applied them for twenty minutes and I did this three times each. I could no longer sleep lying on the left side and each time I moved around even a tiny bit in my bed, the pain woke me up.

Dressing, washing and cooking took up much energy and time, however I found that I was able to compensate somewhat for the limited movement range in my left side by using my right non-dominant hand to, for example, brush my teeth. I had to bend my upper body in order to wash my hair on the left side, since I could not reach that far and I could not lower my head.

I had to keep feeding us, so I mightily struggled in order to keep substitute teaching at the nearby school that allowed me to work half days only. I used my non-dominant arm to write on the board and I laid down in exhaustion on the cold floor as soon as my students were out of the room. By the end of the day, I painfully limped.

CHAPTER 24: "AGRUAR" AND COMMUNICATION CHALLENGES

My hypersensitivity allowed me to pick up subtle data, it felt as if my senses were like a little radar that kept going at all times, whether I wanted it or not. During the next four years I was so raw that I startled and tensed up with the slightest thing. In an attempt to describe with only one word the many things that so intensely made me ill, I made up the word "AGRUAR," for "AGgressive, RUshed and ARtificial." Nowhere did it feel safe, even inside my apartment. I realize that the following may be a bit of an unpleasant litany but this was my life and so I shall describe some of it.

On the scale of sensory challenges, many noises were like an airplane landing near me. Noise was everywhere and unceasing, even during the night as I constantly have a tinnitus buzz inside my ears. Also, the refrigerator's cooling system (and in the winter the heater) intermittently switched on and off during the night. As soon as I woke up, I heard a water pump in the building. During the day, this might be masked by other louder sounds, like when my many neighbors did their laundry, took showers and the old pipes hissed, turned on vacuum cleaners, televisions, stereos, coffee grinders, microwaves, hairdryers, etc. I often believed I heard the phone ringing when it was not, or I heard the alarm clock buzz in my head long after I had turned it off.

I lived near a busy boulevard and the passing traffic of cars and trucks was upsetting, especially when they had a siren on or when a working crew brought loud machinery with backing up warning beeps. At times the bus engines at the nearby bus stop broke with a sharp screech and their electric doors opened and shut with a loud squeak. I braced myself on Monday mornings, when the loud garbage trucks caused the ground to shake and the street sweeper went by. On Thursday mornings, the outside landscaping maintenance staff used the leaf blower or the lawnmower. In the summer, the heat was such that I had to open the windows and these noises intensified. The complex's swimming pool, just outside my door, echoed with the children's chant "Marco Polo," which became imprinted in my brain.

My sense of smell was a second contender for sensory challenges. The laundry room of the complex where I live is not too far from my apartment, and sometimes people used a fragrance whose strong scent seeped under my closed door and gave me an immediate sharp migraine. Many friends of both Matthieu and me habitually had on such artificial fragrances that I just could not have them over. Body lotions and hand creams often contained an ingredient that felt and smelled like a metal; inhaling any of it felt like an iron bar hitting me in the forehead and remaining there. Once, when a service guy came in my apartment with cologne on, the immediate migraine, coupled with gastrointestinal pain, came on me and I tried to go as far as possible in the other room while crying and bent over in pain. When buying liquid soap of any type, it was very easy to make mistakes. Several times I was misled by labels printed in such small letters that I could not read the ingredients, while larger-font letters advertised "for sensitive skin" or "doctor approved." The thought of the poor autistic baby who had to endure this crossed my mind more than once.

Lights were another problem, as almost all artificial lights felt like a knife cutting me; I went to bed almost as soon as the sun went down and if I really had to, especially in the winters, in the evening I turned on one soft light. In the morning I got up before dawn and did not turn any light on, as once my blinds were up the outdoor complex lights were plenty enough for me to see my way around, even for cooking breakfast. Sometimes a neighbor's white light bulb shone directly in my apartment and I had to put a shade in front of it. I hardly ever turned on my computer.

Given how affected I was while inside my apartment, going outside was ten times worse, like being in a war zone. I was constantly assaulted by a cacophony of various stimuli and I was at the mercy of my environment. Vibrations are a constant in present day life as, for example, vehicles of all kinds weigh heavily on the road. Movement is also a constant, with many people herded in big stores, malls, and companies. In waiting rooms, on top of the noise and the light, the constant moving of many people walking around made me nauseous. Even while trying to go to sleep I could feel far away vibrations. I was never able to make sure the next day, but several times I suspected there had been an earthquake somewhere.

When one is rushed, one (including myself) automatically makes more noise: cars and trucks go faster, doors are slammed, lights are quickly turned on, etc. I was so raw that I was often able to perceive that sort of aggressiveness immediately. At least two times while I was so raw, friends spoke to me with such misunderstanding and aggressiveness that, along with nausea and colitis, the pain in my neck immediately intensified. My sciatic nerve was affected and for about two days afterwards I limped and had to use crutches to walk.

Though there are many more, I will only give here two examples of the dangers of such sensory challenges. Once, in a waiting room, a child took out of her mother's purse spray perfume and sprayed with it, which to me was as if she had used a gun. I became physically and mentally paralyzed. Luckily, my son was with me and he took me outside. Another time, when I was the passenger in a car and it was already dark outside, I had to pull down my hat to cover my eyes and it upset the driver next to me as I was then unable to direct him; his upset immediately penetrated to the marrow of my neck and spine.

There was only so much I could do in order to remedy such sensory stress. My bed was in the living room so there was one more wall between it and the nearby avenue traffic, I disabled the phone's ringer. In order to avoid the noise and vibrations of the vacuum cleaner at home, I often scrubbed the carpet in my small apartment by hand. Later, a friend helped me cover the fridge light with black tape so it would not shine so strongly, and he took off all the doors' clicking latches. I sometimes turned on the fan or played a pink-noise CD to try to absorb noises. Last but not least I developed a complex headgear, which is described in the following chapter, and I simply avoided many things.

In the middle of the night when I woke up sick with nervousness, I sometimes felt as if I were on a raft in the middle of a storm with huge waves, hanging on for dear life. Since I did not sleep well at night I was often exhausted during the day. On many days, I lay down all afternoon on the couch in my living room, glad to be able to see the blue sky and the tree. The unbearable and inescapable pain kept me wrapped up in it and put a damper on everything, making it difficult to have space for anything other than it.

I tried my best to mirror Dr. H.'s decision to ignore this unbearable pain, I mightily struggled to invalidate what had become my constant companion. Of course, this inward conflict caused me much mental anguish. I was emotionally troubled, my mind often felt caught into a vortex and I cycled further and further into depression.

Unless they were serious Zen students or in helping professions, few people wanted to have conversations with me as I spoke with such nervous, "pressured speech" about topics they were usually not familiar with such as sensory challenges and unbearable pain in the neck, shoulder and back. When I was so extremely raw most of the people either seemed to feel smug or quickly became uncomfortable. I concluded that pain is a taboo subject and I just felt further despondent. It sometimes just plain hurt to be with others when their ways could be so toxic for me. My behaviors, such as moving away from a fragrance, reflected my pain but people could not see the cause. Many who had never themselves experienced such a thing could become upset by what they thought to be willful, impolite behaviors. I often felt like an unseen seed buried far in the ground and not getting any water. After any inordinately stressful incident I became nauseous, had colitis and gastrointestinal pains, and limped painfully for a few days after.

Sometimes people thought I was crazy and told me so. In light of this, is it any wonder if "emotional insanity" develops?

Mental illness has the potential to affect all of us and we may have to navigate around it, at times closer than others. As Edward Podvoll wrote, "If you have a mind, you can lose it." For many years, it was a not so remote a possibility for me, and during these "dark whirl" years, this was a close call. It seems to me that for some autistic people the line between sanity and insanity might be at times so fine that it becomes extremely easy to be pushed over into the abysses of the mind.

Pursuant to these emotional challenges, my communication was affected. It may be taken for granted that every human being who speaks a second language fluently and has a university diploma, communicates and performs public relations activities with ease and fluidity. But judging from my own experience and that of other autistic adults I know it is not always so.

When I had to complete a form, and especially if I was somewhere else but home, I was often too overwhelmed by the AGRUAR environment to be able to think well. So I often forgot to write about some related relevant matters or the paperwork ended up having many crossed marks. On pre-set forms, I often did not have enough space to be truthful about my inordinate story and I regularly found myself unable to "check the box." For example, in the category about race, those who read the "Caucasian" box I had checked almost always assumed I was born and raised in United States. Or, under the category that lists illnesses, high blood pressure was all the rage and sure to be listed, while low blood pressure was ignored.

When I speak, my logic sometimes goes from A to C, only then returning to B. I may not finish my sentence properly or use the wrong preposition in the wrong order. Sometimes speaking about a subject brings to my mind another thought I don't want to forget so I jump around without explanations and without finishing the original line of thought. Of course then what I actually want to say is often unclear or misunderstood. It is interesting to note that I do the same types of non-sequitur when I speak in French.

Telephone calls to any kind of government agencies were incredibly challenging during these years. First, I had to motivate myself to place the necessary call. I wrote it down on my calendar, and rewrote the reminder note over and over in the next day's slot hoping that I would eventually become so fed up with this procrastination that I would place the call. But before that, I also had to write down carefully what I wanted to say so that I would be able to read it despite the anxiety that tightened my throat.

Finally, during a morning when I felt stronger, I placed what had by now become an absolutely required telephone call. Often there was a long wait and an annoying musical tune played over and over. The longer the wait, the more my nervousness built up. Then there was the actual conversation with a complete stranger who was often rushed. The conversations that followed sometimes scared me even more and my nervousness could be heard in my pressured speech." The more upset I was, the more difficult it was for that person to listen and understand what I was calling about, especially since it was often a long and unusual story. Unable to understand or answer that person, they may become uncomfortable and transfer me, sometimes without informing me—and I then had to speak and explain my "never simple story" all over again to another stranger. Sometimes the person who answered was not more knowledgeable, and I was given the run around or more phone calls had to be made. At any rate, this meant more wait, more static coming from the phone, and more white noise such as when I was put on speaker phone and there was other noise going on in the background which rendered me partially deaf. In any event I often hung up the telephone only to cry and be miserable. When it was an incoming call, however, the tension I felt was much lessened since whoever called me was motivated and may ask questions, rather than me having to explain myself or do the asking.

Writing an email or a letter was often the best form of communication for me then, especially if I could compose my email early in the day, when I had the most energy, I was alone in my apartment, and daylight softened the light issuing from the computer. Because the faint light and the buzz emitted by the computer screen also rendered me ill, I had to be rather quick. Often having to write forced me to put in words thoughts and feelings I might otherwise have kept to myself. But emails, letters or telephone conversations do not allow for in depth communication; they make me think of a sculpture without its depth and relief. I have written many letters to try to connect that were never answered. There is no substitute for spending time with me and for having a direct one-on-one conversation. Through direct contact I am given the chance to take on shape and colors, like a blurry picture which slowly develops into a clearer view.

CHAPTER 25: COPING WITH ILLNESS AND HEADGEAR

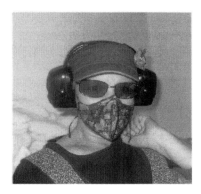

Protective headgear, 2008

During the next three years, the three-day sesshins, organized by my Zen Buddhist group every six months or so, were my only source of group socializing. My limitations were sometimes difficult to understand, such as, for example, when I had to ask for a room all by myself. However the sangha always ended up making the necessary allowances (financially too) for me to participate, a fact for which I am deeply grateful as I have come to realize that these sesshins were a major reason that I remained sane during this dark period of my life. But the Monday night Zen meets caused too much AGRUAR exposure because people usually were unable to realize that their noises, fragrances and the bright lights they turn on were painful to me, and I had to stop going. Instead, I found a Zen Buddhist sangha which met early in the morning. I correctly figured that at such an early hour, it would not be as crowded and there would therefore be fewer stimuli to contend with.

The best means of transportation for me was biking. I able to stave off some AGRUAR that way because it is quieter, there are less fragrances to contend with and I can wear my hat visor low in order to cut down the lights. Also when I sat on the saddle, my weight was supported by the seat and pedals rather than bearing weight on my back. I did not have much strength left in my left fingers and was unable to break with them, so I used only the other hand and it was difficult to balance while mounting on and off my bike. I was careful and very slow on my bike, but at least I was able to schedule doctor appointments, as early as possible and within biking distance. Many of my acquaintances were surprised that I was able to bike despite my illness, but I simply did not have the choice and the physical pain paled in comparison to what I experienced in cars and buses.

A year after I was paralyzed, and three months before he turned sixteen years old, Matthieu organized his own move to a shared apartment several blocks away. He and I never discussed it but as a teenager, who usually likes noise and such, life with me had become impossible in the face of my increasing disability. His departure allowed me to have more time for myself and I increased the amount of time I meditated, practiced yoga and massaged my neck alone at home in the mornings.

I knew it was healthy to go outside and walk a little bit, so about one morning a week I biked over to the nearest trail entrance. I avoided weekends as the hills were then more crowded and I chose the longer but non-trodden paths. My destination was a big oak tree, about thirty minutes away. In order to reach the spacious fork of the big tree, I had to climb on a large low limb. Without the ability to use my upper body and unable to twist and push, I crawled on the branch at a snail pace. But I figured that nobody could see me and I had all the time I needed for it. I brought a thermos of hot tea, an apple, and a cushion so that after a little snack I was able to do zazen in this arboreal refuge.

Even in the hills, the quietness was relative. Often enough, the people I met had a fragrance on or they spoke to one another loudly; or the busy distant boulevard traffic, the wailing fire trucks sirens or the little planes that flew over the area made much noise. Often I had to put back on the earplugs that I had tucked away in my jeans pocket at the beginning of the trail. A few times the weather was too hot and despite my many stops in order to rest, I became dehydrated and had a huge headache for a few hours afterwards. Most of the time the effort paid off and for two or three hours after my time in the tree I had more energy.

In order to go outside, I wore a hat with visor, sunglasses and silicon earplugs—I kept five different sets of them in my small apartment. But I needed better protection and I was unable to afford any extra; the usual face masks were intended to block dirt or germs but they did not repel fragrances. Helpfully, the volunteer who called me once a week in order to support me and Martthieu, and who was a lifesaver at times, sent me a mask with a changeable carbon insert, which did a much better job of it. Her support gave me permission to explore new ideas about preventing sensory overload even though other people thought I was simply crazy.

With the energy of despair I devised a way to strengthen my ear protection. After searching online, I ordered online professional ear-protective headsets, the type sometimes seen on heavy equipment operators. The noise protection they afforded was far from enough, so I figured out a cheap way to enhance them. First, I readied myself by writing down my question, and then I called a soundproofing company to ask if there was a material I could add to the headsets in order to lessen sounds. After the familiar unpleasant comment ("You guys—meaning autistics—exaggerate"), the company agreed to give me scraps of mass-loaded vinyl (MLV), a material used for sound proofing.

In order to get the scraps, I had to pick them up, which was the first of many hurdles. The friends I asked could not understand why I was unable to get them myself. It took a year for a friend to finally pick the MLV scraps up for me. Then, the second hurdle was to cut two patches of the thick material so that I could insert them inside the headsets. I could not do this by myself either as I did not have the strength to use scissors with my dominant hand, the only one that could be used to cut the heavy MLV. When after another few months yet another friend helped me cut and insert the patches. The result was worth it, despite that the project took more than a year to complete.

It was only when I just did not have any other choice that I started to wear this headgear in public. With it on, I was quite the unexpected sight. The visible, chunky, ear protection device set me apart, and was a barrier between me and others. Many people avoided looking at me when I wore it. They sometimes let me know, in no minced words, that they felt I was impolite or crazy, and this is often still going on nowadays only the difference is that I care less. Invisible to all, I wore earplugs under the altered headsets. Even with this gear on, I was so raw that I heard too much. However, the background noises diminished in intensity enough that overtime, when I was in a bus or in a crowded environment, my brain relished the difference. The altered headsets-earplugs combination made it bearable for me to go out in the din of cars, trucks and all the man-made loud constant noises; at times I even wore them in my own apartment.

Ignorant or negative comments felt like poisoned arrows and burning acid. I can't stress enough how the thought of such aggressions deterred me from using this useful, cheap headgear; it went against my deep desire to be unnoticeable. In order to be less offensive, I tried to not wear each piece of this regalia all at once. In fact, they were many instances where I did not wear them when I ought to have done so.

I hope that on some future day, like the blind person's cane or the wheelchair, this headgear will become a usual sight, and the people who are autistics like me—especially children—will not be afraid to protect themselves thus, though their parents will have to be the ones making sure they protect themselves. When I was a child, I had no idea how AGRUAR hurt me. More information about challenges with noise can also be found at www.hyperacusis.net.

CHAPTER 26: MY SEARCH LEADS TO THE DISCOVERY OF AUTISM FOR MYSELF (AND MY FATHER)

Medically, I hoped that a proper understanding of my condition would be identified. After my move to Marin County, I once again subjected myself to various medical exams and tests, all with a common factor. Due to my acute sensory overload and the resulting pain in my neck, the tests were extremely painful and no one was aware of this. It would be tedious to describe how many of the doctors I met with reached gravely incorrect conclusions about me: psychotherapists, physical therapists, endocrinology, acupuncture, osteopath, sleep center studies, hospitals visits, etc.

I will only give the example of the difficulties between Dr. H. and me, which happened despite the fact that Dr. H. was well-intentioned and that I am sure that he has helped many others. After all, to him I did not appear to make sense of this world (I am embarrassed to think about this) and I was unable to let him know how incorrect he was. It could easily have been Dr. A., B., and C., since, for forty-six years, doctors did not correctly recognize my basic problem. During the same years as when I saw Dr. H., I can honestly cite eight other examples of grave misinterpretations by a doctor. Incorrect beliefs are so often encountered by many an autistic individual that they become overwhelming.

I sent several letters to Dr. H. and none were answered. In one of them I wrote "I cannot make it to the clinic due to the physical pain I get into… is there a way to have a consultation in another way? There has to be something planned for people who are too ill to be able to go out." But these words were lost in a bunch of less important information and since Dr. H. did not believe me, he probably did not even go as far as reading these bits of the letter. I probably would have done the same in his shoes. For example, about six years later, when I was much stronger, a non-autistic friend, whom I believed to not be so well in touch with reality, sometimes sent me long emails, and though I usually read them hastily, I did not always read every single one.

On one of my loan discharge applications Dr. H. once commented: "Ms. Davin is completely incapable of rational thinking." He probably wrote this because he believed it would help, but the loan organization had already spoken to me several times, both in writing and on the phone, and they knew very well I was capable of rational thinking. Dr. H. stopped prescribing the medicine I had been given, by another doctor, for my adrenal insufficiency. This was an unexpected surprise, which I only found out at the drugstore one early morning when I went there to get my refill. My French therapist was livid.

Another time, Dr. H. expressed anger that I sat just outside the clinic's front door instead of inside the waiting room as he felt I was being picky and spoiled. It's ironic because I did not like it either; it was often cold and humid on the hard slat without back support, and many of the people who passed by seemed to give me accusatory, somber looks that further made me feel isolated. Lastly, a confused Dr. H. once told me I had abused his staff because when his assistant took my blood pressure prior to a visit, the strong fragrance she had on gave me such a migraine that I had to put on my face mask right in front of her.

I am far from being the only autistic person who has experienced health provider incomprehension, and I do not mean to be accusatory. Misdiagnoses have happened since the beginning of the world, all of us (including me) at times misunderstand the person right next to us. Parents and caregivers of children with autism need to be aware to be extremely cautious before buying into what doctors tell them. Trust that you actually know better the larger picture, and that this matters very much in light of your autistic child. You are often the only person who can protect your child from real danger.

At the same time, the few doctors who were able to go beyond the box helped me move in the right direction, one slow and excruciating step at a time. Dr. Y., at the medical clinic, figured out two major co-morbidities of my autism: the adrenal insufficiency and the orthostatic hypotension. But even the doctors who helped to find about these important pieces of the picture did not figure the root of the problem. They were never really equipped for what was needed for the likes of me, and their ministrations often felt like a drop of water in a vast ocean. My raw hypersensitivities to AGRUAR remained, and I still had many limitations.

When Dr. Y. left the clinic, she steered me to see one of the nurses she felt would be best for me, apparently not knowing that this nurse too was about to leave the clinic. Nevertheless this visit, in the spring of 2008, turned out to be a most important breakthrough. The CalWORKs' case worker, who for the past two years had come with me to many of my doctors' appointments, was also present during this most important visit. This may have been compelling for the nurse; she listened, and the case worker was able to clarify when needed. When the nurse heard me speak about my fainting spells as a teenager and the fact that I attributed them to noise, she thought about Asperger's Syndrome.

I did not know what to do next with this information, so my case worker told me to check it on the Internet, and this is the first thing I did once I was back home. Some of what was written immediately rang deeply true, it was startling and my heart started to pound with excitement. I decided to sleep on it to see if still it would make sense the next day, but I was so excited I could hardly sleep at all. Reviewing everything by the light of what I had read online (and was reading more about), by the next morning, there was no doubt in my mind that I am on the autism spectrum. Later, I realized that what had kept me from guessing I am autistic is in a large part the misconceptions about it that I had. Like many, I incorrectly and ignorantly believed autism to be an aberration, a deficiency in intelligence and something that ought to be cured.

I read every book written about autism that I could put my hands on at the public library near me. Books written by authors who are, themselves, autistic were by far more instructive, and it was truly freeing to learn that many people were like me. Suddenly the pieces of the puzzle of my life came together. With much curiosity, when I reviewed many of my life's experiences and pieced them together in this new light, it suddenly made sense. For example, I remembered how during one of my visits to France, my brother teasingly told me that I sometimes sounded like "Rain Man," the autistic character made famous by actor Dustin Hoffman in the movie. When I realized, in hindsight, that I am indeed autistic, I also realized that my brother's comment was not all that far from the truth.

Another helpful result of informally diagnosing myself as autistic is that at least I was now better able to advocate for myself. Because I knew I was not alone, I did not care as much if I was misunderstood. I found a San Francisco support group for autistic adults, Autism Asperger Syndrome Coalition for Education and Network Development (AASCEND.org). At first, I hoped that I might be less exposed to AGRUAR stimuli if I went to check out one of their affiliates, named Autastics, as it is uniquely composed of people on the autism spectrum. They met once a month in the morning on the south side of San Francisco, and, though it was further than I ever went these days, after some difficulty I was able to find someone to drive me and my headgear to a meeting. But it was really too far and as soon as I had more strength and support I went to AASCEND meetings, which also include parents of autistics and professionals (and included sensory overload, just like everywhere else).

However, when I met other autistic adults like me, it was an eye opening experience. It was like seeing what I may look like from the outside: maybe as a sad and upset person, who spoke about subjects that do not necessarily interest the other person, or who appeared to have compulsive habits, like being a picky eater, or being obsessed with cleanliness or other things—what is often called Obsessive Compulsive Disorder. I realized that the other autistic adults I met often had, like me, attempted to cope and found ways to improve their lifestyle. A large number of them not only appeared "normal," but also had various interests with much depth.

One person who I realized displayed autistic traits was my father. The following is a list of some of the autistic things I remember about him: he did not belong to any social group and almost never took vacations or stayed overnight with friends; he was peculiar and compulsive about some of his things, for example his white clothes, the gift of flowers and purses for my mother, gathering crumbs after meals, or playing a favorite piano tune by ear; he liked to eat the same dish over and over; and he got up early and had a ritualistic morning routine. My father never wanted to be photographed, but taking photographs of others was one of his passions (he often complained that it was difficult to catch me smiling). Later, he painstakingly, and rather obsessively, created seven or eight photo albums in chronological order.

In his last letter to me, my father complains about the noise of the television that my mother liked to watch. When I was a child, he and I were often on the same wave-length and did things together, such as, for example tennis, tea, or card games. It is also interesting to note that my mother's family thought that my father and I belonged to a category apart from themselves, my mother, and my brother. My father had the same facial smirk as me when under duress. This smirk appears like a smile that my father and I put on when we are so overwhelmed with some people's anger at us that it is the only defense we can summon. In several of my relationships, this nervous smile caused havoc as the people who witnessed it misread it to mean that I did not care and enjoyed the situation. Apparently the same thing happened to my father, with much graver consequences for him.

In a faded newspaper article about his trial, dated December 21, 1932, my father is decried for his little smirk. There is a picture of him "smiling," to push the point that my father was a spoiled brat and an object of fear. The journalist, who had sent me the news article, had warned me that there was a lot of yellow journalism about the affair, and unfortunately I have lost contact with him. In any event, my father must have intimately known what it is like to be misunderstood and brought low by the power that other people can yield over our autistic people, without ever realizing that he was, himself, autistic.

CHAPTER 27: SOCIAL SECURITY AND FORMAL DIAGNOSIS

CalWORKS was faithful in their promise to help. When I told them that I am on the autism spectrum, they sent their expert to evaluate me at my home. She saw that I am neurologically different and she had me tested by HHS's onsite consulting psychologist, Dr. S. In order to do this I had to go twice to their office, another extreme tale of pain to which I won't subject the reader. The tests had many silly questions, for example: answer yes or no to the statement "I do not like to wait." At that time in my life it was true that I did not like to wait in public places because the more I waited the more in pain I became. But in reality, I have an inordinate capacity for patience; sitting upright, completely still and without distractions for forty minutes at a time, such as in zazen, fosters patience, among other things.

In any event, these visits paid off and the HHS expert on people with different ways started to write on my behalf her report to Social Security Disability. I do not doubt that her report to the Department of Health and Human Services very much helped, as without it Social Security would probably not have listened. Still, there were many other challenges during the evaluation process. I had to obtain other reports, complete much paperwork, and visit the Social Security office several times. During one of the interviews I was unable to remember my son's date of birth as the question was asked just at the moment when someone behind me laughed noisily. After yet another interview I left in such a daze that I was almost knocked off my bike by a passing car.

But Social Security awarded me a monthly disability allocation and in January 2009, I received their first financial support. I am really grateful for it, as it did come at the very last minute when I was about to collapse for good. It was the beginning of a new phase. At least my minimal living expenses were covered, and since I did not have the strength to go very far (for example I did not see a dentist for about four years), it was just enough to cover the basics. I had my bike checked for maintenance, as I had not been able to do any bike repair for the past four years and the breaks were in danger of completely giving out. With the initial retroactive chunk of money, I was able to afford a hyperbaric oxygen chamber. I craved the energy and the "safe-breathing" feeling of no sudden loud noises. While inside the chamber, it felt like a nest and I was able to sleep! When Dr. H, back at the traditional medical clinic, learned that I had bought a chamber, he called the doctor who sold it to me and accused him of taking advantage of me, but this was far from the truth.

One of the Zen meditation groups I irregularly attended tried to help me. A member started to call me once a week and she helped me write an article entitled "Autism and My Zen Practice," which was published in the December 2010/January 2011 edition of *Common Ground* magazine. For the first time I was heard; it felt like if I had broken the sound barrier.

Last, but not least, the next winter during a rare visit to a Zen event, I met Glen. He was a nurse who is also a Zen monk and he decided to try to help me. For the next two years, he took me to see many doctors. Though Glen and I had several difficult arguments—I was so raw and he did not believe that I was autistic—in the end I am really grateful for his support as it really helped. I could not have done many of the following doctor visits (and more) without Glen's help.

These improvements helped me survive the following "one-and-a-half year of limbo," when I was yet another informally self-diagnosed autistic adult, a frustrating position that many autistic adults know intimately. Beyond not receiving support from any public agency, it often means that friends and family do not believe you have a disability and, instead, they think you are lazy and refuse to help yourself in any way.

Any kind of work had become impossible and for over a year I did not have any health care provider. I sensed that I ought to see a neurologist so, despite my phobia of telephone calls, I called and checked all the neurologists who lived in my area. But none of them took my minimal health insurance and I never dared advocating for myself or broaching the subject of my autism. Of course the inability to obtain a formal diagnosis for autism is due in part to financial and health coverage restrictions, but the lack of understanding, the stigma and false assumptions about it also weigh heavily.

Pursuant to Social Security Disability's awarding, I was automatically enrolled in Medicare a year later. Since this North American health insurance is accepted by many specialists, I could finally see a neurologist. By then, I just was too ill to be able to tackle this task alone. Fortuitously, despite our difficult relationship, my friend Glen managed to hang around and he had the integrity to take me to see a neurologist. I was just absolutely scared, after all no doctor in forty-six years had been able to diagnose my autism, and the numerous traumatic experiences in my entire life regarding my autism were too complex to explain or even remember all that well. I had very little hope that the neurologist would "get me," but I had no choice.

Contrary to what I feared the neurologist was able to "see" me and he gave me a formal diagnosis and told me that I ought to take medicine, which confirmed what I had surmised. Some of the books written by autistic people had helped me overcome my inflexibility toward biochemistry. The neurologist also told me to find a psychiatrist for long term follow up. He asked for MRIs of my neck, brain and left shoulder.

Because my health insurance did not allow me to have the MRIs done all at once, I had to have them done at three separate times. Each time, the MRI room felt to me like a modern chamber of torture. I wore my earplugs and the staff covered my ears with their own protecting device, but the machine's noise nevertheless reverberated *inside* me and my nerves tensed and something inside me shrunk. When I first entered the office, I was walking on my own but I got off the scanner unable to walk. I had to lean on the attendant for support until I could grab my crutches. I endured the terrible procedures with the hope it would help not only me but also others like me.

Disappointingly, not much came out of these MRIs. Dr. B., the psychiatrist who worked in the same building as the neurologist, accepted my insurance and she prescribed Quetiapine (or Seroquel), an antipsychotic medicine which utterly revived me. Only two days after I started to take it, I was able to go with my son to a coffee shop with an outdoor patio, something I had not done in the previous four years. Giddily I noticed that I was no longer made nauseous by the sunlight playing on the leaves.

I am privileged. Because I live independently and do not have to work to earn money, I am able to lead a relatively unencumbered life and I can get by with only a low dose of the antipsychotic medicine. Since I take it just before going to bed the drowsiness affect, with its slurred speech, is actually helpful; it knocks me off for a short three hours or so of sleep. Until then, because my brain was always on the alert and I was often too high-strung to be able to sleep well. But once I started to sleep better, I had more energy during the day and the good sleep at the start of the night calmed me enough that for the remainder of the night sleep kept on happening (despite that I often had nightmares, restless leg syndrome, or woke up regularly when I turned around). At least the deep anxiety-filled dreams were not as intense. I am deeply grateful for sleep, any sleep.

By morning time, the drowsiness is long gone and my morning Zen meditation further wakes my brain up. I find the thought of how truly impaired I would be if I did not meditate distressing: for one I would have to take such a large dose of the antipsychotic medicine that the drowsiness might last throughout the day. Side effects such as weight gain and dry mouth, although very real, seem to me a minor problem when compared to how my life was without the medicine. For those who do not really know about serious neurological impairment, my dosage may seem like a lot; after all, this medicine is very strong. But, in fact, other autistic individuals are often prescribed up to five times the dose.

AFTERWORD: A NEW LEASE ON LIFE

Suddenly, and unexpectedly, I started to recover and my life picked up. I will give an overview of the improvements in the quality of my life after the formal diagnosis.

Only two months after starting the medicine, I was able to attend one of the annual picnics of AASCEND, a San Francisco-based support group for autistic adults, family members and professional who work with them. There I met Greg, the co-president, and we immediately hit it off. Two major interests bound us together as we are both on the spectrum -some of his writings can be found at autismtheory.org- and he practices Zen in the same lineage as me (Soto). A few months later, Greg moved in with me in what used to be my son's room (he now lives nearby), and we now share the cost of the rent. It has been five years and this was completely unexpected. Greg is a handyman and a cancer survivor, and he can only work part-time. Consequently, we are always on a shoe-string budget and we do not have a car, partly by choice, but also because it is too stressful.

Since my psychiatrist was able to properly certify my disability, my student loan discharge application was finally accepted by the U.S. Department of Education. Slowly but surely my newfound energy kept increasing. Not only was I no longer dizzy, it took me three times less to perform the same yoga routine as before and my thresholds to withstand a toxic environment augmented enough that I was progressively able to stop using the hyperbaric oxygen chamber. It was very satisfying to be able to towel myself in the back of my shoulders, or to be able to pass my left arm in the shoulder strap of my backpack without pain.

At home, my morning massage routine gave me much relief over time, and the pain in my neck, spine and elsewhere, at last became bearable. Two years after the formal diagnosis, I had recovered enough strength to find a way to apply for and receive financial help in the form of Patient Assisted Fund, in order to weekly see a chiropractor regularly and receive massage therapy. The Sutter Pacific Health and Healing Institute where I do this therapy work has been particularly patient in the face of slow improvements. My sensory hypersensitivity improved at exactly the same pace as the pain reduction which makes me wonder if these two apparently different symptoms are linked.

Today, the tensed knot in my neck is still present and I have to do a strict daily massage routine at home and alone. At times of extreme sensory overload, I still become overwhelmed and limp but my threshold is much higher and the invisible chronic pain is manageable. Cane, crutches and face mask are put away. It has been almost fifteen years since "The Night" during which the crisis of the nerves in my neck and spine happened—an event I now think may have been predisposed by my odd gait in childhood. I used to be so unaware of what was going on in my body that I just never noticed its pain and discomfort, as evidenced by the fact I rarely knew where bruises on my body came from.

I wonder if hypersensitivity is really the "result" of hidden pain. My chiropractor told my neurologist he has never seen anything like that in his thirty years of practice. Judging by how much more positively people react to me, I seem to communicate more efficiently. Though when I pass a pedestrian on my bike, I must coach myself to say loud enough the "on your left" warning. The constant exchange of thoughts with Greg has often helped me put in words inner thoughts I never shared with anyone. I have become more assertive and am less rocked by aggressive displays.

Mostly, I can't stress enough how fortunate I am to have a Zen meditation practice, it underlies all of the improvements in my life. When I started I had nothing to lose—so why not sit still for a while with some discipline and regularity? Sitting zazen never directly made my pain go away, and at times it was just the opposite as it made me more aware of it. But in the long run, it helped me face the grim reality in a calmer way and find an unexpected clarity of mind. I do not doubt that it is the reason that I kept my sanity and self-respect, at a time when so many people believed I had lost it. I spend more and more time sitting upright, still and quiet on my round black cushion, and find one of the most important improvements in my life is that I now can go practice with others more often.

What started as a miserable and solitary life slowly developed over the years into a life I could not have imagined was possible, and I am curious to see where my life will take me. Though I must be very careful to lead a quiet life, and I still cannot work much outside, my present well-being is a continuous source of wonder to me. Recently, I started a blog in order to promote this book, Autizen.com. Thank you for taking the time to read my book. I hope it helps.

ABOUT THE AUTHOR

Anlor (from *Anne-Laure*) Davin is autistic. She was diagnosed at age 46, a life-changing, and life-saving, event she traces to her Zen practice of the years preceding. Anlor is an immigrant, born in France in 1964. During Anlor's childhood her native France was in the grip of oppressive and now discredited theories about autism. Anlor instinctively knew she had to flee France in order to survive.

Upon arrival to the Unites States in 1987, Anlor lived in Chicago, Illinois, were she married and had a son. The ensuing eighteen years of child-rearing, a tremendous challenge for an autistic mother, over-whelmed her and her life slowly but surely unraveled. Forever searching for answers to the challenges of an undiagnosed autistic life she moved to San Francisco, California, in 1999. There she started a Zen practice while she eventually became very ill and "hit bottom." In March 2000 a painful and debilitating movement disorder appeared in her left upper body.

Anlor was finally formally diagnosed in 2010. With proper medical care and many other supports her life improved unexpectedly and dra-matically. This healthy outcome and Anlor's later fullness of life give her a secure place to stand and reflect with greater clarity on her journey. She now lives near San Francisco with her partner, her son living nearby.